Ketogenic Mediterranean Diet Cookbook for Beginners

600-Day Low-Carb, High-Fat Keto Recipes for Delicious Mediterranean Diet to Burns Fat, Promotes Longevity, and Prevents Chronic Disease

Baelry Jinms

© Copyright 2021 Baelry Jinms - All Rights Reserved.

In no way is it legal to reproduce, duplicate, or transmit any part of this document by either electronic means or in printed format. Recording of this publication is strictly prohibited, and any storage of this material is not allowed unless with written permission from the publisher. All rights reserved.

The information provided herein is stated to be truthful and consistent, in that any liability, regarding inattention or otherwise, by any usage or abuse of any policies, processes, or directions contained within is the solitary and complete responsibility of the recipient reader. Under no circumstances will any legal liability or blame be held against the publisher for any reparation, damages, or monetary loss due to the information herein, either directly or indirectly.

Respective authors own all copyrights not held by the publisher.

Legal Notice:

This book is copyright protected. This is only for personal use. You cannot amend, distribute, sell, use, quote or paraphrase any part of the content within this book without the consent of the author or copyright owner. Legal action will be pursued if this is breached.

Disclaimer Notice:

Please note the information contained within this document is for educational and entertainment purposes only. Every attempt has been made to provide accurate, up-to-date and reliable, complete information. No warranties of any kind are expressed or implied. Readers acknowledge that the author is not engaging in the rendering of legal, financial, medical or professional advice.

By reading this document, the reader agrees that under no circumstances are we responsible for any losses, direct or indirect, which are incurred as a result of the use of information contained within this document, including, but not limited to, errors, omissions, or inaccuracies.

Table of contents

Introduction 6
Chapter 1: Mediterranean Diet Basic 7
    What is the Mediterranean diet? 7
    The history of the Mediterranean diet? 7
    The Science Behind Mediterranean diet 8
    Benefits of the Mediterranean diet 8
Chapter 2: Keto Diet Basics 10
    What is Keto Diet? 10
    How does Keto Diet Work? 10
    How to Know Whether Your Body is in Ketosis or Not? 10
    The Advantages of Keto Diet 12
    Tips and Tricks for Successful Keto Journey 13
Chapter 3: Breakfast & Brunch 15
    Rosemary Broccoli Cauliflower Mash 15
    Vegetable Quinoa 16
    Zucchini Pudding 17
    Quinoa Breakfast Bowls 18
    Garlic Potatoes 19
    Mushroom Cheese Breakfast 20
    Chia Carrot Oatmeal 21
    Perfect Breakfast Oatmeal 22
    Pear Breakfast Rice 23
    Simple Lemon Quinoa 24
    Potato Cheese Frittata 25
Chapter 4: Soups & Stews 26
    Healthy Vegetable Soup 26
    Tomato Chickpeas Stew 27
    Nutritious Kidney Bean Soup 28
    Easy & Delicious Beef Stew 29
    Celery Soup 30
    Cabbage Soup 31
    Roasted Tomatoes Soup 32
    Spinach Chicken Stew 33
    Curried Zucchini Soup 34
    Easy Cauliflower Soup 35
    Pepper Pumpkin Soup 36
Chapter 5: Pasta, Grains & Beans 37
    Curried Beans 37
    Perfect Herb Rice 38
    Flavors Herb Risotto 39
    Delicious Chicken Pasta 40
    Salsa Chicken Rice 41
    Chicken Risotto 42
    Corn Risotto 43
    Brown Rice Pilaf 44
    Creamy & Tasty Risotto 45
    Flavors Taco Rice Bowl 46
    Tasty Salsa Beans 47
Chapter 6: Vegetables 48

Greek Cauliflower Rice 48
Garlic Basil Zucchini................ 49
Creamy Dill Potatoes 50
Carrot Potato Medley 51
Feta Green Beans.................. 52
Rosemary Garlic Zucchini 53
Creamy Lemon Bell Peppers 54
Potato Salad 55
Radish & Asparagus 56
Spicy Cauliflower 57
Spicy Zucchini.................................. 58

Chapter 7: Appetizers 59
Sausage Queso Dip 59
Kidney Bean Spread..................... 60
Cheesy Corn Dip 61
Spicy Pepper Eggplant Spread 62
Chocolate Hummus........................ 63
Flavorful Roasted Baby Potatoes 64
Slow Cooked Cheesy Artichoke Dip.. 65
Easy Tomato Dip 66
Spicy Chicken Dip............................. 67
Pinto Bean Dip 68
Pepper Tomato Eggplant Spread........ 69

Chapter 8: Poultry.. 70
Flavorful Cafe Rio Chicken................ 70
One Pot Chicken & Potatoes............. 71
Flavorful Mediterranean Chicken 72
Cheese Garlic Chicken & Potatoes.... 73
Tasty Turkey Chili 74
Easy Chicken Scampi......................... 75
Lemon Olive Chicken 76
Easy Chicken Piccata 77
Moroccan Spiced Chicken 78
Shredded Greek Chicken 79
Delicious Gyro Chicken 80

Chapter 9: Beef 81
Flavorful Beef Bourguignon 81
Cauliflower Tomato Beef.................... 82
Delicious Beef Chili............................ 83
Moist Shredded Beef......................... 84
Beef Curry... 85
Delicious Ground Beef...................... 86
Hearty Beef Ragu 87
Sage Tomato Beef 88
Beef Shawarma................................... 89
Rosemary Beef Eggplant 90
Lemon Basil Beef................................ 91

Chapter 10: Pork 92
Walnut Pork Chops............................ 92
Lime Salsa Pork Chops 93
Pork Roast with Potatoes 94
Pork with Vegetables......................... 95
Pork with Beans 96
Pork Rice... 97
Cheese Pork Chops 98
Capers Pork Chops............................ 99
Garlic Parsley Pork Chops 100
Pork with Carrots Potatoes............... 101
Simple Shredded Pork 102

Chapter 11: Lamb.. 103
Delicious Salsa Lamb 103
Sweet Potato lamb 104

Healthy Quinoa Lamb 105
Tomato Oregano Lamb Stew............ 106
Italian Lamb Stew 107
Lamb Stew.. 108
Tomato Lamb Chops....................... 109
Flavors Lamb Ribs 110
Mediterranean Lamb 111
Curried Lamb Stew.......................... 112
Garlic Coriander Lamb Chops......... 113

Chapter 12: Seafood & Fish 114

Pesto Fish Fillet................................ 114
Delicious Lemon Butter Cod 115
Quick & Easy Shrimp...................... 116
Italian White Fish Fillets 117
Shrimp Scampi................................. 118
Honey Garlic Shrimp....................... 119
Feta Tomato Sea Bass 120
Lemon Cod Peas.............................. 121
Spicy Tomato Crab Mix 122
Chili Lime Salmon 123
Lemoney Prawns 124

Chapter 13: Desserts 125

Apple Dates Mix 125
Fruit Nut Bowl 126
Chocolate Nut Spread 127
Raisins Cinnamon Peaches 128
Choco Rice Pudding 129
Healthy Zucchini Pudding............... 130
Coconut Risotto Pudding................. 131
Strawberry Stew............................... 132
Tapioca Pudding.............................. 133
Blackberry Jam 134
Spiced Pear Sauce 135

Conclusion 136

Introduction

The Ketogenic Mediterranean diet is widely acknowledged to be among the very best in the world for losing fat rapidly and promoting optimal health. Many people associate keto with eating a high fat diet. Keto works well on its own, but when combined with the Mediterranean diet, it becomes the ultimate way to lose fat and promote longevity and overall well-being. Sticking to a diet is never easy and getting started can be the hardest part of all. Make it easy on yourself by grabbing this cookbook and enjoying a variety of the very best Ketogenic Mediterranean meals for health, longevity, and weight loss that you can make tonight in your own kitchen!

Combining the Ketogenic lifestyle with the Mediterranean diet has been proven as a healthy and effective way to achieve your weight loss goals while still enjoying some of the best tasting food you've ever served at home. Grab this Ketogenic Mediterranean Diet Cookbook today and see for yourself what kind of amazing Ketogenic Mediterranean dishes you can make tonight!

Chapter 1: Mediterranean Diet Basic

Mediterranean diet is not just a diet plan it is one of the healthy eating lifestyles. Most of the scientific study and research conducted over the Mediterranean diet proves that the Mediterranean diet helps to reduce your excess weight, cancer cell reduction and also reduces the risk of cardiovascular diseases.

Most of the scientific study also proves that the food consumption during the Mediterranean diet like vegetables, whole grain, nuts, fish and seasonable fruits improves blood vessels functions and reduce the risk of metabolic syndrome.

What is the Mediterranean diet?

Mediterranean diet is one of the traditional diets comes from different Mediterranean countries and regions. Mediterranean diet is basically a plant-based diet that allows you high consumption of vegetables, fruits, nuts, beans, grains, fish and olive oil. Mediterranean diet is a rich fat diet, it allows near about 40 percent of calories from fat. It also allows for consuming a moderate amount of protein and low consumption of meat and dairy products.

Mediterranean diet linked with good health and a healthier heart, it helps to reduce your health issues like diabetes and heart-related disease.

The history of the Mediterranean diet?

Mediterranean diet is one of the oldest diets plans popular in worldwide. It is near about more than three thousand years old diet plan. Mediterranean is the name of the sea situated between Asia, Europe and Africa. Mediterranean diet is an eating habit of people's lives around the coast of the Mediterranean Sea like Italy, France, Spain, Greece and Morocco. There are near about 22 countries situated near the Mediterranean Sea. The large amounts of seasonable fruits are available during four seasons because of mild climate.

There are large numbers of olive trees found in Mediterranean regions. Near about 90 percent of the world, olive trees are grown in Mediterranean regions. Due to large sea coast fishing is the main occupation by most of the people in this region and fish is part of the Mediterranean diet. Most of the scientific study conducted over Mediterranean diet proves that the diet helps to reduce the all-cause mortality. It also reduces the risk of heart-related disease and early death.

The Science Behind Mediterranean diet

Mediterranean diet is one of the high-fat diets that allow near about 40 percent of calories from fat. It is the most studied and healthiest diet worldwide.

The scientific research and study show that the peoples who follow the Mediterranean diet have lower the risk of cardiac mortality and heart disease. The study shows that the Mediterranean diet is a high-fat dietduring the diet, our body consumes a high intake of unsaturated fat and low intake of saturated fat. Unsaturated fats help to increase the HDL (Good Cholesterol) level into your body. Olive oil is one of the main fats used during the Mediterranean diet. Olive oils are full of monounsaturated fats that help to control your diabetes. It improves your insulin sensitivity and controls your diabetes. If you don't have diabetes then it helps to reduce the risk of developing diabetes.

Another study shows that the Mediterranean diet reduces the risk of stomach cancer and also reducing the risk of breast cancer in women.

Benefits of the Mediterranean diet

Mediterranean diet is one of the oldest diets in the world comes with various types of health benefits. Some of the important benefits are as follows.

- **Improves heart health**

During the Mediterranean diet, olive oil is used as a primary fat. This olive oil contains healthy fat known as monounsaturated fat helps to increase the HDL (Good Cholesterol) level and reduce the LDL (Bad Cholesterol) level. Fish is also part of the Mediterranean lifestyle, fish contains Omega-3 fatty acid which helps to improve the heart health and reduce the risk of heart failure, strokes, and sudden cardiac death.

- **Help to maintain blood sugar level**

According to the American Heart Association, the Mediterranean diet is low in sugar. It is very effective in type-2 diabetes patients and helps to maintain the blood sugar level. Mediterranean diet is rich in monounsaturated fats which help to reduce the cholesterol level and maintain your blood sugar level.

- **Increase your lifespan**

Mediterranean region's climate is clear and pollution-free climate. Due to this, you have to find fresh vegetables, seasonable fruits, beans, olives and fish in this region. All of the natural and fresh foods are full of antioxidants, which helps to reduce the inflammation in your body and slow down your aging process. It also reduces the risk of heart-related disease, inflammation, Alzheimer's and depression. The peoples live in Mediterranean regions have a longer lifespan.

- **Protects from cancer**

Mediterranean diet is one of the simple plant-based food diet. It allows high fat moderate protein and low consumption of red meat. Most of the scientific study and research show that reduction of red meat from your diet and increase the consumption of olive oil and fish into your daily diet will help to reduce the risk of several common cancers. Fish contains omega-3 fatty acids which reduce the risk of cancer.

- **Fight against depression**

The foods associated with the Mediterranean diet have anti-inflammatory properties which help to reduce the depression and help to improve your mood. One of the scientific research studies shows that the peoples who follow the Mediterranean diet have 98.6 percent of lower the risk of depression.

Chapter 2: Keto Diet Basics

What is Keto Diet?

The Keto diet is one of the most effective and popular diet plans comes with long term health benefits. Keto is a low-carb, high-fat diet plan that allows a moderate amount of protein during the diet period. Keto is not just a diet plan it completely changes your daily food eating habit towards natural and healthy food consumption. Generally, our body depends on glucose (carb) for energy to perform day-to-day activities. When the glucose level in our body increases the excess glucose is converted into glycogens and stored in liver and body cells.

The Keto diet is a low carb diet, so the carb consumption is reduced during a keto diet. Due to this glucose level is decreased and our body finds out the alternative source for energy. It breaks down fats for energy. This state of the body is also called ketosis. It is one of the metabolic processes where fats are broken down and produce ketones for energy. These ketones provide an endless source of energy to our body. The Keto diet is one of the most followed diets for weight loss purposes. It not only maintains your healthy body weight but also improves your physical and mental health.

How does Keto Diet Work?

In general, our body uses glucose (carb) as a primary source of energy. When we reduce the intake of carbohydrates during the diet, glucose level automatically reduces. In this condition, our body shifts itself to break down fats for energy in the absence of carbohydrates (glucose). In fat breaking process some fatty acids are released our livers convert these fatty acids into ketones.

Ketones are produced due to a chemical process when our body burns fat for energy instead of glucose. Most of the body organs and tissues use these ketones as an alternative source of energy. Ketones are one of the best fuels for our brain they fulfill more than 70% of our brain energy needs. The lack of glucose pushes our body into the state of ketosis.

How to Know Whether Your Body is in Ketosis or Not?

There are several sign and symptoms and methods which indicate that your body is in the state of ketosis or not. These signs, symptoms, and methods are mention as follows.

- **Increase in thirst and dry mouth**

This is one of the common side effects noticed when you are following a keto diet. In this state, your body loses excess sodium and water, so it is recommended that add 2 to 4 grams of sodium into your diet to balancing the electrolyte level into your body. This will also increase the urination process and increase thirst. These signs and symptoms indicate that your body is in a state of ketosis.

- **Keto Breath or Bad Breath**

This is one of the common side effects noticed during the first week of the keto diet. When your body breaks down fats for energy, in this process acetone are release and produce a fruity smell or nail polish remover like smell having the bad breath symptoms. This is happening due to keto diet plan adaptation. Keto breath or bad breath symptoms will indicate that your body is in the state of ketosis.

- **Rapid Weight Loss**

This happens when your body breaks down fats for energy instead of glucose (carb). If you notice that your weight is rapidly reduced during the first week of the keto diet, then. Rapid weight loss is another sign and symptom that indicates that your body is in the state of ketosis.

- **Blood Test**

A blood test is one of the common and accurate methods used to measure the ketones level. It is one of the few expensive methods of measuring blood ketones levels in diabetic patients. The blood test method is similar to a glucometer test. In this case, you need to use a keto meter instead of a glucometer with a lancet pen and test strips. If the keto meter shows reading 0.5 and 3 mml/L which indicates that your body is in the state of ketosis.

- **Ketostix**

Ketostix is one of the accurate and inexpensive ways to check your ketones level in the urine. You just need to collect the urine in a clean urine container then dip the Ketostix and shake to remove the excess urine from the stick and wait for 15 seconds. After 15 minutes you have noticed that Ketostix color is changed. To measure the ketones level just follow the color guide match with your strip color to check the ketosis.

- Increase focus and energy

Most people notice that tiredness and sickness during the first few days of the keto diet. When your body uses ketones for energy. It not only improves your physical health but also improves your focus and energy. This is happening because 70% of brain energy needs are fulfilled by ketones. This is another sign which indicates that your body is in the state of ketosis.

The Advantages of Keto Diet

The keto diet is one of the most popular diets for years comes with various kinds of health benefits some of them are described as follows.

- Rapid Weight loss

If you are overweight and want to reduce the extra weight rapidly then the keto diet is one of the best choices to maintain your healthy body weight. During the keto diet, our body breaks down fats for energy instead of glucose. Due to this fat breaking process, you have notice rapid weight loss. The diet allows a moderate number of proteins, so you don't feel hungrier during the diet period. This will help to reduce your bodyweight rapidly and gives you long term weight loss benefits.

- Improve your Brain Functions

Keto diet is low carb diet, due to low carb consumption glucose level decreases and our body finds out alternative energy source by breaking the fats for energy. During the fat breaking process some chemical releases. Our liver converts these chemicals into ketones. To perform day-to-day operations our body use ketones as an energy source. It fulfills more than 70% of brain energy needs. Most of the study and research proves that ketones improve focus, attention and memory functions.

- Effective on various medical conditions

The keto diet is not only used for weight loss purposes but also used to treat various medical conditions like Alzheimer's, Parkinson's, type-2 diabetes, heart-related disease, blood pressure, and also in epilepsy conditions.

- Improves Cholesterol Levels

The keto diet is a low-carb high-fat diet. It allows you to consume healthy fats during the diet period. Healthy fats are responsible to improve the HDL (good cholesterol) level. Carbohydrates are one of the main reasons to increase the LDL (bad cholesterol) level. The Keto diet is a low-carb diet, so it decreases the LDL level and also reduces the risk of heart-related disease.

- **Control Appetite**

The keto diet is a low carb, high fat, and moderate protein diet. The diet is enriching with all essential nutrients the moderate protein in diet which helps prevent an increase in appetite. You never feel hungry after eating healthy keto diet food.

- **Longevity**

Keto diet is responsible to increase your lifespan. The keto diet allows you to consume healthy notorious and antioxidant-rich foods. This will help to cures various health-related problems that occur due to the consumption of unhealthy and poor diet. The scientific studies prove that the peoples who follow the keto diet can result in a significant drop in oxidative stress level. It also reduces the risk of diabetes, heart disease, and obesity and improves lifespan.

- **Increase in energy levels**

The keto diet shifts your body to breakdown fats for energy instead of glucose. During the fat breaking, process chemicals are released, and our liver converts it into ketones. Ketones provide energy to our body organ and tissues and long-lasting energy source to our body. Due to an increase in energy level, you feel active and fully energized the whole day.

Tips and Tricks for Successful Keto Journey

The following tips and tricks are helpful to complete your keto journey.

1. **Limit Daily Carb Consumption**

To stay in ketosis, it is recommended to consume 10 to 30 grams of carb daily. If you are an active person and doing hard exercise for 5 to 6 days a week then you can increase carb consumption. Don't eat too much carb it may build up glycogen storage.

2. **Eat healthy fats**

During the keto diet, it is recommended to eat healthy fats like avocado oil, olive oil, coconut oil, etc. avoid unhealthy fats like vegetable oil, sunflower oil, canola oil, etc.

Healthy fat consumption will help to boost ketone levels in your body and keep your body in a ketosis state.

3. **Get enough sleep**

Due to Inadequate sleep, you feel hunger and it is one of the bad signs for your weight loss process. To stay in ketosis during the keto diet you need not only enough sleep but also get better quality sleep. Better quality means you should sleep in a cool and darkroom. The room temperature is maintained at 65 F and you need to sleep at least 7 hours a daily night to get complete enough sleep.

4. **Consume Moderate Protein**

In the keto diet our body breaks down fats for energy. In this fat breaking process some healthy muscles and fats. An adequate amount of protein consumption will help to repair this muscle and also maintain muscle mass. As per your body weight, it is recommended to consume 0.75 grams of protein per pound.

5. **Regular exercise**

Regular exercise during the keto diet will keep you energized throughout the day. It also increases the ketones level and decreases the carb from your body. Regular exercise keeps you fit and also maintains your blood sugar level.

6. **Use MCT oils**

Use coconut oil which contains healthy fats called MCT (Medium Chain Triglycerides). It is easily absorbed by the liver and converts into ketones. MCT oils provide an instant source of energy to our body and are converted into ketones. MCTs travel fast into your body and enter into your body cells without broken.

7. **Stay Hydrated**

When you follow the keto diet, it is important to keep your body hydrated. During the diet period, your body loses glycogens through the urination process. These glycogens hold 5 parts of water, so your body is dehydrated during the diet. To keep your body hydrated you need to consume smoothies, coffee, or tea during the diet period.

Chapter 3: Breakfast & Brunch

Rosemary Broccoli Cauliflower Mash

Preparation Time: 10 minutes
Cooking Time: 12 minutes
Serve: 3

Ingredients:
- 2 cups broccoli, chopped
- 1 lb cauliflower, cut into florets
- 1 tsp dried rosemary
- 1/4 cup olive oil
- 1 tsp garlic, minced
- Salt

Directions:
1. Add broccoli and cauliflower into the instant pot. Pour enough water into the pot to cover broccoli and cauliflower.
2. Seal pot with lid and cook on high for 12 minutes.
3. Once done, allow to release pressure naturally. Remove lid.
4. Drain broccoli and cauliflower well and clean the instant pot.
5. Add oil into the pot and set the pot on sauté mode.
6. Add broccoli, cauliflower, rosemary, garlic, and salt and cook for 10 minutes.
7. Mash the broccoli and cauliflower mixture using a potato masher until smooth.
8. Serve and enjoy.

Nutritional Value (Amount per Serving):
- Calories 205
- Fat 17.2 g
- Carbohydrates 12.6 g
- Sugar 4.7 g
- Protein 4.8 g
- Cholesterol 0 mg

Vegetable Quinoa

Preparation Time: 10 minutes
Cooking Time: 1 minute
Serve: 6

Ingredients:

- 1 cup quinoa, rinsed and drained
- 1 1/2 cups water
- 4 cups spinach, chopped
- 1 bell pepper, chopped
- 2 carrots, chopped
- 1 celery stalk, chopped
- 1/3 cup feta cheese, crumbled
- 1/2 cup olives, sliced
- 1/3 cup pesto
- 2 tomatoes, chopped
- Pepper
- Salt

Directions:

1. Add quinoa, spinach, bell pepper, carrots, celery, water, pepper, and salt into the instant pot and stir well.
2. Seal pot with lid and cook on high for 1 minute.
3. Once done, allow to release pressure naturally for 10 minutes then release remaining using quick release. Remove lid.
4. Add remaining ingredients and stir everything well.
5. Serve and enjoy.

Nutritional Value (Amount per Serving):

- Calories 226
- Fat 10.7 g
- Carbohydrates 26 g
- Sugar 4.4 g
- Protein 7.9 g
- Cholesterol 11 mg

Zucchini Pudding

Preparation Time: 10 minutes
Cooking Time: 10 minutes
Serve: 4

Ingredients:

- 2 cups zucchini, grated
- 1/2 tsp ground cardamom
- 1/4 cup swerve
- 5 oz half and half
- 5 oz unsweetened almond milk
- Pinch of salt

Directions:

1. Spray instant pot from inside with cooking spray.
2. Add all ingredients into the instant pot and stir well.
3. Seal pot with lid and cook on high for 10 minutes.
4. Once done, allow to release pressure naturally for 10 minutes then release remaining using quick release. Remove lid.
5. Stir well and serve.

Nutritional Value (Amount per Serving):

- Calories 62
- Fat 4.7 g
- Carbohydrates 18.9 g
- Sugar 16 g
- Protein 1.9 g
- Cholesterol 13 mg

Quinoa Breakfast Bowls

Preparation Time: 10 minutes
Cooking Time: 4 minutes
Serve: 4

Ingredients:

- 1 cup quinoa, rinsed and drained
- 1 cucumber, chopped
- 1 red bell pepper, chopped
- 1/2 cup olives, pitted and sliced
- 1 tbsp fresh basil, chopped
- 2 tbsp fresh lemon juice
- 1 tsp lemon zest, grated
- 1 1/2 cups water
- Pepper
- Salt

Directions:

1. Add quinoa, lemon zest, lemon juice, water, pepper, and salt into the instant pot and stir well.
2. Seal pot with lid and cook on high for 4 minutes.
3. Once done, allow to release pressure naturally for 10 minutes then release remaining using quick release. Remove lid.
4. Add remaining ingredients and stir well.
5. Serve immediately and enjoy it.

Nutritional Value (Amount per Serving):

- Calories 199
- Fat 4.6 g
- Carbohydrates 33.6 g
- Sugar 3 g
- Protein 7 g
- Cholesterol 0 mg

Garlic Potatoes

Preparation Time: 10 minutes
Cooking Time: 5 minutes
Serve: 2

Ingredients:
- 1 lb potatoes, cut into chunks
- 2 tbsp fresh parsley, chopped
- 1/4 cup vegetable stock
- 1 tsp garlic, minced
- 1 tbsp olive oil
- Pepper
- Salt

Directions:
1. Add oil in instant pot and set the pot on sauté mode.
2. Add garlic, potatoes, and salt and sauté for 5 minutes. Add stock and stir well.
3. Seal pot with lid and cook on high for 5 minutes.
4. Once done, release pressure using quick release. Remove lid.
5. Garnish with parsley and serve.

Nutritional Value (Amount per Serving):
- Calories 221
- Fat 7.3 g
- Carbohydrates 36.5 g
- Sugar 2.7 g
- Protein 4.1 g
- Cholesterol 0 mg

Mushroom Cheese Breakfast

Preparation Time: 10 minutes
Cooking Time: 12 minutes
Serve: 4

Ingredients:

- 5 eggs
- 2 tbsp olive oil
- 1 onion, chopped
- 2 tbsp chives, minced
- 1 1/2 cups mushrooms, sliced
- 1/2 cup almond milk
- 1/2 tbsp cheddar cheese
- 1 bell pepper, chopped
- Pepper
- Salt

Directions:

1. Add oil into the instant pot and set the pot on sauté mode.
2. Add mushrooms and sauté for 2 minutes. Transfer mushrooms on a plate and clean the instant pot.
3. In a bowl, whisk eggs with pepper and salt. Add mushrooms, onion, chives, almond milk, cheese, and bell pepper into the egg mixture and whisk well.
4. Spray baking dish with cooking spray.
5. Pour 1 1/2 cups of water into the instant pot then place steamer rack in the pot.
6. Pour egg mixture into the prepared baking dish. Cover dish with foil.
7. Place baking dish on top of the steamer rack.
8. Seal pot with lid and cook on high for 10 minutes.
9. Once done, release pressure using quick release. Remove lid.
10. Serve and enjoy.

Nutritional Value (Amount per Serving):

- Calories 238
- Fat 20.1 g
- Carbohydrates 7.9 g
- Sugar 4.6 g
- Protein 9.3 g
- Cholesterol 206 mg

Chia Carrot Oatmeal

Preparation Time: 10 minutes
Cooking Time: 10 minutes
Serve: 6

Ingredients:
- 1 cup steel-cut oats
- 1/4 cup chia seeds
- 1 cup carrot, grated
- 1 1/2 tsp ground cinnamon
- 4 cups almond milk

Directions:
1. Spray instant pot from inside with cooking spray.
2. Add all ingredients except chia seeds into the instant pot and stir well.
3. Seal pot with lid and cook on high for 10 minutes.
4. Once done, allow to release pressure naturally for 10 minutes then release remaining using quick release. Remove lid.
5. Stir in chia seeds and serve.

Nutritional Value (Amount per Serving):
- Calories 434
- Fat 39.4 g
- Carbohydrates 20.9 g
- Sugar 6.4 g
- Protein 5.8 g
- Cholesterol 0 mg

Perfect Breakfast Oatmeal

Preparation Time: 10 minutes
Cooking Time: 4 minutes
Serve: 4

Ingredients:

- 1 cup steel-cut oats
- 3/4 cup unsweetened shredded coconut
- 1/4 tsp ground ginger
- 1/4 tsp ground nutmeg
- 1/2 tsp ground cinnamon
- 1/4 cup raisins
- 1 apple, chopped
- 1 1/2 cup carrots, shredded
- 1 cup unsweetened almond milk
- 3 cups of water

Directions:

1. Add all ingredients except raisins and shredded coconut into the instant pot and stir well.
2. Seal pot with lid and cook on high for 4 minutes.
3. Once done, allow to release pressure naturally. Remove lid.
4. Stir well and top with raisins and shredded coconut and serve.

Nutritional Value (Amount per Serving):

- Calories 297
- Fat 14.4 g
- Carbohydrates 38.2 g
- Sugar 14.9 g
- Protein 5.2 g
- Cholesterol 0 mg

Pear Breakfast Rice

Preparation Time: 10 minutes
Cooking Time: 15 minutes
Serve: 4

Ingredients:
- 1 1/2 cups rice
- 3 cups almond milk
- 2 pears, cored and sliced
- 2 tbsp maple syrup
- 1 tsp ground cinnamon

Directions:
1. Spray instant pot from inside with cooking spray.
2. Set instant pot on sauté mode. Add rice and sauté for 5 minutes.
3. Add remaining ingredients except for maple syrup and stir well.
4. Seal pot with lid and cook on high for 10 minutes.
5. Once done, allow to release pressure naturally for 10 minutes then release remaining using quick release. Remove lid.
6. Stir in maple syrup and serve.

Nutritional Value (Amount per Serving):
- Calories 755
- Fat 43.6 g
- Carbohydrates 88.5 g
- Sugar 22.2 g
- Protein 9.5 g
- Cholesterol 0 mg

Simple Lemon Quinoa

Preparation Time: 10 minutes
Cooking Time: 1 minute
Serve: 4

Ingredients:

- 2 cups quinoa, rinsed and drained
- 1 fresh lemon juice
- 2 tbsp fresh parsley, chopped
- 3 cups of water
- 1/4 tsp salt

Directions:

1. Spray instant pot from inside with cooking spray.
2. Add all ingredients except lemon juice and parsley into the pot. Stir well.
3. Seal pot with lid and cook on high for 1 minute.
4. Once done, allow to release pressure naturally for 10 minutes then release remaining using quick release. Remove lid.
5. Add parsley and lemon juice.
6. Stir and serve.

Nutritional Value (Amount per Serving):

- Calories 317
- Fat 5.3 g
- Carbohydrates 54.9 g
- Sugar 0.3 g
- Protein 12.2 g
- Cholesterol 0 mg

Potato Cheese Frittata

Preparation Time: 10 minutes
Cooking Time: 10 minutes
Serve: 2

Ingredients:

- 6 eggs
- 1/2 cup cheddar cheese, shredded
- 1/4 cup almond milk
- 1/2 small onion, chopped
- 1/2 bell pepper, chopped
- 1 small potato, peeled and chopped
- Pepper
- Salt

Directions:

1. Pour 1 cup of water into the instant pot then place the steamer rack in the pot.
2. In a bowl, whisk eggs with pepper and salt. Add remaining ingredients and stir well.
3. Spray heat-safe dish with cooking spray.
4. Pour egg mixture into the prepared dish and place dish on top of the steamer rack.
5. Seal pot with lid and cook on high for 10 minutes.
6. Once done, release pressure using quick release. Remove lid.
7. Serve and enjoy.

Nutritional Value (Amount per Serving):

- Calories 454
- Fat 29.8 g
- Carbohydrates 21.8 g
- Sugar 5.1 g
- Protein 26.6 g
- Cholesterol 521 mg

Chapter 4: Soups & Stews

Healthy Vegetable Soup

Preparation Time: 10 minutes
Cooking Time: 15 minutes
Serve: 4

Ingredients:
- 1 cup can tomatoes, chopped
- 1 small zucchini, diced
- 3 oz kale, sliced
- 1 tbsp garlic, chopped
- 5 button mushrooms, sliced
- 2 carrots, peeled and sliced
- 2 celery sticks, sliced
- 1/2 red chili, sliced
- 1 onion, diced
- 1 tbsp olive oil
- 1 bay leaf
- 4 cups vegetable stock
- 1/4 tsp salt

Directions:
1. Add oil into the inner pot of instant pot and set the pot on sauté mode.
2. Add carrots, celery, onion, and salt and cook for 2-3 minutes.
3. Add mushrooms and chili and cook for 2 minutes.
4. Add remaining ingredients and stir everything well.
5. Seal pot with lid and cook on high for 10 minutes.
6. Once done, allow to release pressure naturally for 10 minutes then release remaining using quick release. Remove lid.
7. Stir well and serve.

Nutritional Value (Amount per Serving):
- Calories 100
- Fat 3.8 g
- Carbohydrates 15.1 g
- Sugar 6.6 g
- Protein 3.5 g
- Cholesterol 0 mg

Tomato Chickpeas Stew

Preparation Time: 10 minutes
Cooking Time: 25 minutes
Serve: 4

Ingredients:

- 1 lb can chickpeas, rinsed and drained
- 18 oz can tomatoes, chopped
- 1/2 tsp red pepper flakes
- 2 tbsp olive oil
- 1 tsp dried oregano
- 1 tsp garlic, minced
- 1 onion, chopped
- Pepper
- Salt

Directions:

1. Add oil into the inner pot of instant pot and set the pot on sauté mode.
2. Add onion and garlic and sauté for 5 minutes.
3. Add remaining ingredients and stir well.
4. Seal pot with lid and cook on high pressure 20 for minutes.
5. Once done, allow to release pressure naturally for 10 minutes then release remaining using quick release. Remove lid.
6. Serve and enjoy.

Nutritional Value (Amount per Serving):

- Calories 236
- Fat 8.4 g
- Carbohydrates 35.3 g
- Sugar 5.6 g
- Protein 7.2 g
- Cholesterol 0 mg

Nutritious Kidney Bean Soup

Preparation Time: 10 minutes
Cooking Time: 1 hour 40 minutes
Serve: 8

Ingredients:

- 3 cups red kidney beans, soaked overnight & drain
- 1/4 cup fresh parsley, chopped
- 6 cups of water
- 1/4 cup olive oil
- 1 1/2 tbsp tomato paste
- 2 bell peppers, chopped
- 2 carrots, chopped
- 1 tbsp garlic, minced
- 1 onion, chopped
- 1 tsp salt

Directions:

1. Add oil into the inner pot of instant pot and set the pot on sauté mode.
2. Add garlic and onion and sauté until onion is softened.
3. Add carrots and bell peppers and sauté for 3-5 minutes.
4. Add beans, parsley, tomato paste, water, and salt and stir everything well.
5. Seal pot with lid and cook on high for 1 hour 40 minutes.
6. Once done, release pressure using quick release. Remove lid.
7. Stir well and serve.

Nutritional Value (Amount per Serving):

- Calories 312
- Fat 7.2 g
- Carbohydrates 48.4 g
- Sugar 4.7 g
- Protein 16.4 g
- Cholesterol 0 mg

Easy & Delicious Beef Stew

Preparation Time: 10 minutes
Cooking Time: 30 minutes
Serve: 4

Ingredients:

- 1 1/2 lbs beef stew meat, cut into cubed
- 1/2 cup sweet corn
- 1 cup can tomato, crushed
- 1 cup chicken stock
- 4 carrots, chopped
- 1 onion, chopped
- 1 tbsp olive oil
- Pepper
- Salt

Directions:

1. Add oil into the inner pot of instant pot and set the pot on sauté mode.
2. Add onion and meat and sauté for 5 minutes.
3. Add remaining ingredients and stir well.
4. Seal pot with lid and cook on high pressure 25 for minutes.
5. Once done, allow to release pressure naturally for 10 minutes then release remaining using quick release. Remove lid.
6. Stir and serve.

Nutritional Value (Amount per Serving):

- Calories 410
- Fat 14.4 g
- Carbohydrates 14 g
- Sugar 4.8 g
- Protein 54.4 g
- Cholesterol 152 mg

Celery Soup

Preparation Time: 10 minutes
Cooking Time: 30 minutes
Serve: 4

Ingredients:

- 6 cups celery stalk, chopped
- 1 cup heavy cream
- 1 onion, chopped
- 2 cups vegetable broth
- 1/2 tsp dill
- Salt

Directions:

1. Add all ingredients into the instant pot and stir well.
2. Seal pot with lid and cook on high for 30 minutes.
3. Once done, release pressure using quick release. Remove lid.
4. Blend soup using an immersion blender until smooth.
5. Serve and enjoy.

Nutritional Value (Amount per Serving):

- Calories 158
- Fat 12.1 g
- Carbohydrates 8.4 g
- Sugar 3.6 g
- Protein 4.4 g
- Cholesterol 41 mg

Cabbage Soup

Preparation Time: 10 minutes
Cooking Time: 7 minutes
Serve: 4

Ingredients:
- 3 cups cabbage, chopped
- 2 tbsp olive oil
- 5 oz tomato paste
- 14.5 oz can stewed tomatoes
- 1/2 onion, sliced
- 1 tbsp garlic, diced
- 14. oz can tomatoes, diced
- 4 cups vegetable stock
- Pepper
- Salt

Directions:
1. Add oil into the inner pot of instant pot and set the pot on sauté mode.
2. Add onion and garlic and sauté for 2 minutes.
3. Add cabbage, water, tomato paste, and tomatoes. Stir well.
4. Seal pot with lid and cook on high for 5 minutes.
5. Once done, allow to release pressure naturally for 5 minutes then release remaining using quick release. Remove lid.
6. Serve and enjoy.

Nutritional Value (Amount per Serving):
- Calories 165
- Fat 7.5 g
- Carbohydrates 24.1 g
- Sugar 14.3 g
- Protein 4.7 g
- Cholesterol 0 mg

Roasted Tomatoes Soup

Preparation Time: 10 minutes

Cooking Time: 5 minutes

Serve: 2

Ingredients:

- 14 oz can fire-roasted tomatoes
- 1 1/2 cups vegetable stock
- 1/4 cup zucchini, grated
- 1/2 tsp dried oregano
- 1/2 tsp dried basil
- 1/2 cup heavy cream
- 1/2 cup parmesan cheese, grated
- 1 cup cheddar cheese, grated
- Pepper
- Salt

Directions:

1. Add tomatoes, stock, zucchini, oregano, basil, pepper, and salt into the instant pot and stir well.
2. Seal pot with lid and cook on high for 5 minutes.
3. Once done, release pressure using quick release. Remove lid.
4. Set pot on sauté mode. Add heavy cream, parmesan cheese, and cheddar cheese and stir well and cook until cheese is melted.
5. Serve and enjoy.

Nutritional Value (Amount per Serving):

- Calories 460
- Fat 34.8 g
- Carbohydrates 13.5 g
- Sugar 6 g
- Protein 24.1 g
- Cholesterol 117 mg

Spinach Chicken Stew

Preparation Time: 10 minutes
Cooking Time: 25 minutes
Serve: 4

Ingredients:

- 2 cups spinach, chopped
- 1 lb chicken breasts, skinless, boneless, and cut into chunks
- 1/2 cup can tomato, crushed
- 1 cup chicken stock
- 1 onion, chopped
- 1 tbsp olive oil
- Pepper
- Salt

Directions:

1. Add oil into the inner pot of instant pot and set the pot on sauté mode.
2. Add chicken and onion and sauté for 5 minutes.
3. Add remaining ingredients and stir well.
4. Seal pot with lid and cook on low for 20 minutes.
5. Once done, allow to release pressure naturally for 10 minutes then release remaining using quick release. Remove lid.
6. Stir well and serve.

Nutritional Value (Amount per Serving):

- Calories 266
- Fat 12.2 g
- Carbohydrates 4.2 g
- Sugar 1.4 g
- Protein 33.9 g
- Cholesterol 101 mg

Curried Zucchini Soup

Preparation Time: 10 minutes
Cooking Time: 10 minutes
Serve: 6

Ingredients:

- 10 cups zucchini, chopped
- 4 cups vegetable broth
- 14 oz coconut milk
- 1 tsp curry powder
- Pepper
- Salt

Directions:

1. Add all ingredients into the instant pot and stir well.
2. Seal pot with lid and cook on high for 10 minutes.
3. Once done, release pressure using quick release. Remove lid.
4. Blend soup using an immersion blender until smooth.
5. Serve and enjoy.

Nutritional Value (Amount per Serving):

- Calories 209
- Fat 17.1 g
- Carbohydrates 10.8 g
- Sugar 5.9 g
- Protein 7.1 g
- Cholesterol 0 mg

Easy Cauliflower Soup

Preparation Time: 10 minutes
Cooking Time: 30 minutes
Serve: 4

Ingredients:
- 2 cups cauliflower florets
- 3 tbsp olive oil
- 1 onion, chopped
- 1 tsp pumpkin pie spice
- 5 cups chicken broth
- 1/4 tsp salt

Directions:
1. Add oil into the inner pot of instant pot and set the pot on sauté mode.
2. Add onion and sauté for 5 minutes.
3. Add remaining ingredients and stir well.
4. Seal pot with lid and cook on high for 25 minutes.
5. Once done, release pressure using quick release. Remove lid.
6. Blend soup using an immersion blender until smooth.
7. Serve and enjoy.

Nutritional Value (Amount per Serving):
- Calories 163
- Fat 12.3 g
- Carbohydrates 6.7 g
- Sugar 3.3 g
- Protein 6.6 g
- Cholesterol 0 mg

Pepper Pumpkin Soup

Preparation Time: 10 minutes
Cooking Time: 6 minutes
Serve: 6

Ingredients:

- 2 cups pumpkin puree
- 1 onion, chopped
- 4 cups vegetable broth
- 1/4 tsp nutmeg
- 1/4 cup red bell pepper, chopped
- 1/8 tsp thyme, dried
- 1/2 tsp salt

Directions:

1. Add all ingredients into the instant pot and stir well.
2. Seal pot with lid and cook on high for 6 minutes.
3. Once done, allow to release pressure naturally for 5 minutes then release remaining using quick release. Remove lid.
4. Blend soup using an immersion blender until smooth.
5. Serve and enjoy.

Nutritional Value (Amount per Serving):

- Calories 63
- Fat 1.2 g
- Carbohydrates 9.4 g
- Sugar 4.2 g
- Protein 4.4 g
- Cholesterol 0 mg

Chapter 5: Pasta, Grains & Beans

Curried Beans

Preparation Time: 10 minutes
Cooking Time: 1 hour 30 minutes
Serve: 6

Ingredients:

- 2 cups brown rice
- 2 cups dry white beans
- 1/4 cup onion, diced
- 1 sweet potato, peeled and sliced
- 10 cups vegetable stock
- 1 tsp coriander powder
- 1 tbsp curry powder
- 1/2 tsp garlic, minced
- 1 tsp red pepper flakes
- 1 tbsp salt

Directions:

1. Add all ingredients into the inner pot of instant pot and stir well.
2. Seal pot with lid and cook on high for 1 hour 30 minutes.
3. Once done, allow to release pressure naturally. Remove lid.
4. Stir well and serve.

Nutritional Value (Amount per Serving):

- Calories 487
- Fat 2.7 g
- Carbohydrates 95.6 g
- Sugar 4.1 g
- Protein 21.8 g
- Cholesterol 0 mg

Perfect Herb Rice

Preparation Time: 10 minutes
Cooking Time: 4 minutes
Serve: 4

Ingredients:

- 1 cup brown rice, rinsed
- 1 tbsp olive oil
- 1 1/2 cups water
- 1/2 cup fresh mix herbs, chopped
- 1 tsp salt

Directions:

1. Add all ingredients into the inner pot of instant pot and stir well.
2. Seal pot with lid and cook on high for 4 minutes.
3. Once done, allow to release pressure naturally for 10 minutes then release remaining using quick release. Remove lid.
4. Stir well and serve.

Nutritional Value (Amount per Serving):

- Calories 264
- Fat 9.9 g
- Carbohydrates 36.7 g
- Sugar 0.4 g
- Protein 7.3 g
- Cholesterol 0 mg

Flavors Herb Risotto

Preparation Time: 10 minutes
Cooking Time: 15 minutes
Serve: 4

Ingredients:

- 2 cups of rice
- 2 tbsp parmesan cheese, grated
- 3.5 oz heavy cream
- 1 tbsp fresh oregano, chopped
- 1 tbsp fresh basil, chopped
- 1/2 tbsp sage, chopped
- 1 onion, chopped
- 2 tbsp olive oil
- 1 tsp garlic, minced
- 4 cups vegetable stock
- Pepper
- Salt

Directions:

1. Add oil into the inner pot of instant pot and set the pot on sauté mode.
2. Add garlic and onion and sauté for 2-3 minutes.
3. Add remaining ingredients except for parmesan cheese and heavy cream and stir well.
4. Seal pot with lid and cook on high for 12 minutes.
5. Once done, allow to release pressure naturally for 10 minutes then release remaining using quick release. Remove lid.
6. Stir in cream and cheese and serve.

Nutritional Value (Amount per Serving):

- Calories 514
- Fat 17.6 g
- Carbohydrates 79.4 g
- Sugar 2.1 g
- Protein 8.8 g
- Cholesterol 36 mg

Delicious Chicken Pasta

Preparation Time: 10 minutes
Cooking Time: 17 minutes
Serve: 4

Ingredients:

- 3 chicken breasts, skinless, boneless, cut into pieces
- 9 oz whole-grain pasta
- 1/2 cup olives, sliced
- 1/2 cup sun-dried tomatoes
- 1 tbsp roasted red peppers, chopped
- 14 oz can tomatoes, diced
- 2 cups marinara sauce
- 1 cup chicken broth
- Pepper
- Salt

Directions:

1. Add all ingredients except whole-grain pasta into the instant pot and stir well.
2. Seal pot with lid and cook on high for 12 minutes.
3. Once done, allow to release pressure naturally. Remove lid.
4. Add pasta and stir well. Seal pot again and select manual and set timer for 5 minutes.
5. Once done, allow to release pressure naturally for 5 minutes then release remaining using quick release. Remove lid.
6. Stir well and serve.

Nutritional Value (Amount per Serving):

- Calories 615
- Fat 15.4 g
- Carbohydrates 71 g
- Sugar 17.6 g
- Protein 48 g
- Cholesterol 100 mg

Salsa Chicken Rice

Preparation Time: 10 minutes
Cooking Time: 12 minutes
Serve: 8

Ingredients:

- 1 lb chicken breasts, skinless, boneless, and cut into chunks
- 1 tbsp taco seasoning
- 14 oz can black beans, drained and rinsed
- 12 oz frozen corn
- 14 oz salsa
- 3 cups rice, rinsed and drained
- 3 cups vegetable broth
- 1/4 cup cheddar cheese, shredded
- Pepper
- Salt

Directions:

1. Add all ingredients except cheese into the instant pot and stir well.
2. Seal pot with lid and cook on high for 12 minutes.
3. Once done, release pressure using quick release. Remove lid.
4. Add cheese and stir well.
5. Serve and enjoy.

Nutritional Value (Amount per Serving):

- Calories 693
- Fat 11.9 g
- Carbohydrates 114.6 g
- Sugar 9.8 g
- Protein 37.6 g
- Cholesterol 61 mg

Chicken Risotto

Preparation Time: 10 minutes
Cooking Time: 12 minutes
Serve: 4

Ingredients:

- 1 lb chicken breasts, skinless, boneless, and cut into chunks
- 3 tbsp fresh parsley, chopped
- 1/3 cup parmesan cheese, grated
- 1 cup of rice
- 2 cups chicken stock
- 1 cup mushrooms, sliced
- 1 cup onion, diced
- 2 tbsp olive oil

Directions:

1. Add oil into the inner pot of instant pot and set the pot on sauté mode.
2. Add chicken and cook for 3 minutes.
3. Add mushrooms and onions and cook for 2 minutes.
4. Add remaining ingredients except for cheese and stir well.
5. Seal pot with lid and cook on high for 7 minutes.
6. Once done, release pressure using quick release. Remove lid.
7. Stir well and serve.

Nutritional Value (Amount per Serving):

- Calories 490
- Fat 17.7 g
- Carbohydrates 41.1 g
- Sugar 2 g
- Protein 39.8 g
- Cholesterol 106 mg

Corn Risotto

Preparation Time: 10 minutes
Cooking Time: 12 minutes
Serve: 4

Ingredients:

- 1 cup of rice
- 3 cups vegetable broth
- 1 tbsp olive oil
- 1 tsp garlic, minced
- 1 onion, chopped
- 3/4 cup sweet corn
- 1 red pepper, diced
- 1 tsp dried mix herbs
- 1/4 tsp pepper
- 1/2 tsp salt

Directions:

1. Add oil into the inner pot of instant pot and set the pot on sauté mode.
2. Add onion and garlic and sauté for 5 minutes.
3. Add the rest of the ingredients and stir well.
4. Seal pot with lid and cook on high for 8 minutes.
5. Once done, release pressure using quick release. Remove lid.
6. Stir well and serve.

Nutritional Value (Amount per Serving):

- Calories 304
- Fat 5.3 g
- Carbohydrates 54.5 g
- Sugar 4.7 g
- Protein 9.5 g
- Cholesterol 0 mg

Brown Rice Pilaf

Preparation Time: 10 minutes
Cooking Time: 27 minutes
Serve: 6

Ingredients:

- 1 1/2 cups brown rice, rinsed and drained
- 2 tbsp parsley, chopped
- 1 3/4 cups vegetable broth
- 1 tsp garlic, minced
- 1/2 cup onion, diced
- 2 tbsp olive oil
- 1/2 tsp salt

Directions:

1. Add oil into the inner pot of instant pot and set the pot on sauté mode.
2. Add onion and sauté for 5 minutes.
3. Add the rest of the ingredients except parsley and stir well.
4. Seal pot with lid and cook on high for 22 minutes.
5. Once done, allow to release pressure naturally. Remove lid.
6. Garnish with parsley and serve.

Nutritional Value (Amount per Serving):

- Calories 228
- Fat 6.4 g
- Carbohydrates 37.6 g
- Sugar 0.6 g
- Protein 5.2 g
- Cholesterol 0 mg

Creamy & Tasty Risotto

Preparation Time: 10 minutes

Cooking Time: 7 minutes

Serve: 4

Ingredients:

- 2 cups of rice
- 1/2 cup mozzarella cheese, shredded
- 1 cup parmesan cheese, shredded
- 4 cups vegetable stock
- 1/2 cup wine
- 1 small onion, chopped
- 2 tbsp olive oil
- Salt

Directions:

1. Add oil into the inner pot of instant pot and set the pot on sauté mode.
2. Add onion and sauté for 2 minutes.
3. Add rice, wine, stock, and salt and stir well.
4. Seal pot with lid and cook on high for 5 minutes.
5. Once done, release pressure using quick release. Remove lid.
6. Add cheeses and stir until cheese is melted.
7. Serve and enjoy.

Nutritional Value (Amount per Serving):

- Calories 517
- Fat 13.2 g
- Carbohydrates 78.2 g
- Sugar 1.8 g
- Protein 15.4 g
- Cholesterol 18 mg

Flavors Taco Rice Bowl

Preparation Time: 10 minutes
Cooking Time: 14 minutes
Serve: 8

Ingredients:

- 1 lb ground beef
- 8 oz cheddar cheese, shredded
- 14 oz can red beans
- 2 oz taco seasoning
- 16 oz salsa
- 2 cups of water
- 2 cups brown rice
- Pepper
- Salt

Directions:

1. Set instant pot on sauté mode.
2. Add meat to the pot and sauté until brown.
3. Add water, beans, rice, taco seasoning, pepper, and salt and stir well.
4. Top with salsa. Seal pot with lid and cook on high for 14 minutes.
5. Once done, release pressure using quick release. Remove lid.
6. Add cheddar cheese and stir until cheese is melted.
7. Serve and enjoy.

Nutritional Value (Amount per Serving):

- Calories 464
- Fat 15.3 g
- Carbohydrates 48.9 g
- Sugar 2.8 g
- Protein 32.2 g
- Cholesterol 83 mg

Tasty Salsa Beans

Preparation Time: 10 minutes
Cooking Time: 40 minutes
Serve: 6

Ingredients:

- 20 oz package ham pinto beans, rinsed
- 1 jalapeno pepper, diced
- 1 onion, diced
- 5 cups vegetable broth
- 1/4 cup parsley, chopped
- 1/2 cup salsa
- 1/2 tsp garlic, chopped
- Pepper
- Salt

Directions:

1. Add all ingredients into the inner pot of instant pot and stir well.
2. Seal pot with lid and cook on high for 40 minutes.
3. Once done, allow to release pressure naturally. Remove lid.
4. Stir well and serve.

Nutritional Value (Amount per Serving):

- Calories 147
- Fat 2.3 g
- Carbohydrates 27.6 g
- Sugar 2.1 g
- Protein 12.5 g
- Cholesterol 0 mg

Chapter 6: Vegetables

Greek Cauliflower Rice

Preparation Time: 10 minutes
Cooking Time: 12 minutes
Serve: 2

Ingredients:

- 1/2 cup cauliflower rice
- 1 tbsp pecans, toasted and chopped
- 1/2 tbsp fresh lime juice
- 1 1/3 cup vegetable stock
- 3 oz spinach, chopped
- 1/4 cup water
- 1 tbsp olive oil
- 1/2 small onion, chopped
- 1/2 tsp garlic, minced
- 1/4 cup grape tomatoes, halved
- 2 tbsp feta cheese, crumbled
- Salt

Directions:

1. Add oil into the inner pot of instant pot and set the pot on sauté mode.
2. Add garlic and onion and sauté for 5 minutes.
3. Add cauliflower rice, water, and stock and stir well.
4. Seal pot with lid and cook on high for 4 minutes.
5. Once done, release pressure using quick release. Remove lid.
6. Add spinach and tomatoes and cook on sauté mode for 3 minutes.
7. Add remaining ingredients and stir well and serve.

Nutritional Value (Amount per Serving):

- Calories 176
- Fat 14.8 g
- Carbohydrates 8.9 g
- Sugar 3.8 g
- Protein 5 g
- Cholesterol 8 mg

Garlic Basil Zucchini

Preparation Time: 10 minutes
Cooking Time: 8 minutes
Serve: 4

Ingredients:

- 14 oz zucchini, sliced
- 1/4 cup fresh basil, chopped
- 1/2 tsp red pepper flakes
- 14 oz can tomatoes, chopped
- 1 tsp garlic, minced
- 1/2 onion, chopped
- 1/4 cup feta cheese, crumbled
- 1 tbsp olive oil
- Salt

Directions:

1. Add oil into the inner pot of instant pot and set the pot on sauté mode.
2. Add onion and garlic and sauté for 2 minutes.
3. Add remaining ingredients except feta cheese and stir well.
4. Seal pot with lid and cook on high for 6 minutes.
5. Once done, allow to release pressure naturally. Remove lid.
6. Top with feta cheese and serve.

Nutritional Value (Amount per Serving):

- Calories 99
- Fat 5.7 g
- Carbohydrates 10.4 g
- Sugar 6.1 g
- Protein 3.7 g
- Cholesterol 8 mg

Creamy Dill Potatoes

Preparation Time: 10 minutes
Cooking Time: 20 minutes
Serve: 4

Ingredients:

- 2 lbs potatoes, peeled and cut into chunks
- 1 tbsp fresh dill, chopped
- 1 cup vegetable stock
- 3/4 cup heavy cream
- Pepper
- Salt

Directions:

1. Add all ingredients into the inner pot of instant pot and stir well.
2. Seal pot with lid and cook on high for 20 minutes.
3. Once done, allow to release pressure naturally for 10 minutes then release remaining using quick release. Remove lid.
4. Stir and serve.

Nutritional Value (Amount per Serving):

- Calories 238
- Fat 8.6 g
- Carbohydrates 37 g
- Sugar 2.8 g
- Protein 4.5 g
- Cholesterol 31 mg

Carrot Potato Medley

Preparation Time: 10 minutes
Cooking Time: 15 minutes
Serve: 6

Ingredients:

- 4 lbs baby potatoes, clean and cut in half
- 1 1/2 lbs carrots, cut into chunks
- 1 tsp Italian seasoning
- 1 1/2 cups vegetable broth
- 1 tbsp garlic, chopped
- 1 onion, chopped
- 2 tbsp olive oil
- Pepper
- Salt

Directions:

1. Add oil into the inner pot of instant pot and set the pot on sauté mode.
2. Add onion and sauté for 5 minutes.
3. Add carrots and cook for 5 minutes.
4. Add remaining ingredients and stir well.
5. Seal pot with lid and cook on high for 5 minutes.
6. Once done, allow to release pressure naturally for 10 minutes then release remaining using quick release. Remove lid.
7. Stir and serve.

Nutritional Value (Amount per Serving):

- Calories 283
- Fat 5.6 g
- Carbohydrates 51.3 g
- Sugar 6.6 g
- Protein 10.2 g
- Cholesterol 1 mg

Feta Green Beans

Preparation Time: 10 minutes
Cooking Time: 15 minutes
Serve: 4

Ingredients:

- 1 1/2 lbs green beans, trimmed
- 1/4 cup feta cheese, crumbled
- 28 oz can tomatoes, crushed
- 2 tsp oregano
- 1 tsp cumin
- 1/2 cup water
- 1 tbsp olive oil
- 1 tbsp garlic, minced
- 1 onion, chopped
- 1 lb baby potatoes, clean and cut into chunks
- Pepper
- Salt

Directions:

1. Add oil into the inner pot of instant pot and set the pot on sauté mode.
2. Add onion and garlic and sauté for 3-5 minutes.
3. Add remaining ingredients except feta cheese and stir well.
4. Seal pot with lid and cook on high for 10 minutes.
5. Once done, allow to release pressure naturally for 5 minutes then release remaining using quick release. Remove lid.
6. Top with feta cheese and serve.

Nutritional Value (Amount per Serving):

- Calories 234
- Fat 6.1 g
- Carbohydrates 40.7 g
- Sugar 10.7 g
- Protein 9.7 g
- Cholesterol 8 mg

Rosemary Garlic Zucchini

Preparation Time: 10 minutes
Cooking Time: 3 minutes
Serve: 2

Ingredients:

- 2 zucchini, cut into lengthwise
- 3 tbsp parmesan cheese, grated
- 1/2 cup water
- 1/2 tsp dried basil
- 1/4 tsp dried rosemary
- 2 tbsp olive oil
- 1/4 tsp garlic powder
- Pepper
- Salt

Directions:

1. Pout water into the instant pot.
2. Toss zucchini with oil, basil, rosemary, garlic, pepper, and salt.
3. Transfer zucchini into the steamer basket and place basket in the pot.
4. Seal pot with lid and cook on high for 3 minutes.
5. Once done, release pressure using quick release. Remove lid.
6. Transfer zucchini on a plate.
7. Top with cheese and serve.

Nutritional Value (Amount per Serving):

- Calories 177
- Fat 16 g
- Carbohydrates 7.2 g
- Sugar 3.5 g
- Protein 4.9 g
- Cholesterol 5 mg

Creamy Lemon Bell Peppers

Preparation Time: 10 minutes
Cooking Time: 15 minutes
Serve: 4

Ingredients:
- 1 lb bell peppers, cut into strips
- 1 tbsp chives, chopped
- 1 tbsp fresh lime juice
- 1/2 cup heavy cream
- 1/4 tsp dried mix herbs
- Pepper
- Salt

Directions:
1. Add all ingredients into the inner pot of instant pot and stir well.
2. Seal pot with lid and cook on high for 15 minutes.
3. Once done, allow to release pressure naturally for 5 minutes then release remaining using quick release. Remove lid.
4. Stir and serve.

Nutritional Value (Amount per Serving):
- Calories 72
- Fat 5.7 g
- Carbohydrates 5.2 g
- Sugar 1.8 g
- Protein 0.9 g
- Cholesterol 21 mg

Potato Salad

Preparation Time: 10 minutes
Cooking Time: 10 minutes
Serve: 8

Ingredients:
- 5 cups potato, cubed
- 1/4 cup fresh parsley, chopped
- 1/4 tsp red pepper flakes
- 1 tbsp olive oil
- 1/3 cup mayonnaise
- 1/2 tbsp oregano
- 2 tbsp capers
- 3/4 cup feta cheese, crumbled
- 1 cup olives, halved
- 3 cups of water
- 3/4 cup onion, chopped
- Pepper
- Salt

Directions:
1. Add potatoes, onion, and salt into the instant pot.
2. Seal pot with lid and cook on high for 3 minutes.
3. Once done, release pressure using quick release. Remove lid.
4. Remove potatoes from pot and place in a large mixing bowl.
5. Add remaining ingredients and stir everything well.
6. Serve and enjoy.

Nutritional Value (Amount per Serving):
- Calories 152
- Fat 9.9 g
- Carbohydrates 13.6 g
- Sugar 2.1 g
- Protein 3.5 g
- Cholesterol 15 mg

Radish & Asparagus

Preparation Time: 10 minutes
Cooking Time: 8 minutes
Serve: 4

Ingredients:

- 3/4 cup radishes, halved
- 1 lb asparagus, trimmed & cut in half
- 1 tsp chili powder
- 1 tsp lemon zest, grated
- 2 tbsp green onion, chopped
- 2 tbsp olive oil
- Pepper
- Salt

Directions:

1. Add all ingredients into the inner pot of instant pot and stir well.
2. Seal pot with lid and cook on high for 8 minutes.
3. Once done, allow to release pressure naturally for 5 minutes then release remaining using quick release. Remove lid.
4. Stir and serve.

Nutritional Value (Amount per Serving):

- Calories 90
- Fat 7.3 g
- Carbohydrates 5.8 g
- Sugar 2.7 g
- Protein 2.8 g
- Cholesterol 0 mg

Spicy Cauliflower

Preparation Time: 10 minutes
Cooking Time: 6 minutes
Serve: 2

Ingredients:

- 1/2 small cauliflower head, cut into florets
- 1 tbsp fresh parsley, chopped
- 1/2 cup water
- 1/4 tsp paprika
- 1/4 tsp turmeric
- 1/2 tsp ground cumin
- 1 tbsp olive oil
- 1/4 tsp chili powder
- 1/4 small onion, chopped
- 1 tomato, chopped
- Pepper
- Salt

Directions:

1. Add tomato, onion, and chili powder into the blender and blend until smooth.
2. Add oil into the inner pot of instant pot and set the pot on sauté mode.
3. Add blended tomato mixture into the pot and cook for 2-3 minutes.
4. Add paprika, cumin, turmeric, and pepper and stir for a minute.
5. Add remaining ingredients and stir well.
6. Seal pot with lid and cook on high for 3 minutes.
7. Once done, release pressure using quick release. Remove lid.
8. Stir and serve.

Nutritional Value (Amount per Serving):

- Calories 97
- Fat 7.5 g
- Carbohydrates 7.6 g
- Sugar 3.7 g
- Protein 2.2 g
- Cholesterol 0 mg

Spicy Zucchini

Preparation Time: 10 minutes
Cooking Time: 5 minutes
Serve: 4

Ingredients:

- 4 zucchini, cut into 1/2-inch pieces
- 1 cup of water
- 1/2 tsp Italian seasoning
- 1/2 tsp red pepper flakes
- 1 tsp garlic, minced
- 1 tbsp olive oil
- 1/2 cup can tomato, crushed
- Salt

Directions:

1. Add water and zucchini into the instant pot.
2. Seal pot with lid and cook on high for 2 minutes.
3. Once done, release pressure using quick release. Remove lid.
4. Drain zucchini well and clean the instant pot.
5. Add oil into the inner pot of instant pot and set the pot on sauté mode.
6. Add garlic and sauté for 30 seconds.
7. Add remaining ingredients and stir well and cook for 2-3 minutes.
8. Serve and enjoy.

Nutritional Value (Amount per Serving):

- Calories 69
- Fat 4.1 g
- Carbohydrates 7.9 g
- Sugar 3.5 g
- Protein 2.7 g
- Cholesterol 0 mg

Chapter 7: Appetizers

Sausage Queso Dip

Preparation Time: 10 minutes
Cooking Time: 18 minutes
Serve: 8

Ingredients:

- 1 lb Italian sausage, crumbled
- 4 cups Monterey jack cheese, shredded
- 12 oz milk
- 1/4 cup pickles peppers, diced
- 3.5 oz can olives, drained and sliced
- 14.5 oz can tomatoes, diced
- 1 small onion, chopped

Directions:

1. Set instant pot on sauté mode. Add sausage to the pot and cook for 3 minutes.
2. Add onion and sauté for 5 minutes.
3. Add remaining ingredients except for cheese and stir well and cook for 5 minutes.
4. Add shredded cheese and cook for 5 minutes or until cheese is melted.
5. Stir everything well and serve.

Nutritional Value (Amount per Serving):

- Calories 458
- Fat 35.8 g
- Carbohydrates 6.8 g
- Sugar 4.4 g
- Protein 27.1 g
- Cholesterol 102 mg

Kidney Bean Spread

Preparation Time: 10 minutes
Cooking Time: 18 minutes
Serve: 4

Ingredients:

- 1 lb dry kidney beans, soaked overnight and drained
- 1 tsp garlic, minced
- 2 tbsp olive oil
- 1 tbsp fresh lemon juice
- 1 tbsp paprika
- 4 cups vegetable stock
- 1/2 cup onion, chopped
- Pepper
- Salt

Directions:

1. Add beans and stock into the instant pot.
2. Seal pot with lid and cook on high for 18 minutes.
3. Once done, allow to release pressure naturally. Remove lid.
4. Drain beans well and reserve 1/2 cup stock.
5. Transfer beans, reserve stock, and remaining ingredients into the food processor and process until smooth.
6. Serve and enjoy.

Nutritional Value (Amount per Serving):

- Calories 461
- Fat 8.6 g
- Carbohydrates 73 g
- Sugar 4 g
- Protein 26.4 g
- Cholesterol 0 mg

Cheesy Corn Dip

Preparation Time: 10 minutes
Cooking Time: 10 minutes
Serve: 6

Ingredients:
- 4 ears corn
- 1/4 cup fresh basil, minced
- 1/4 cup fresh cilantro, minced
- 1 tbsp fresh lime juice
- 1/4 tsp cayenne
- 1/2 tsp cumin
- 1/2 tsp garlic powder
- 1 tsp paprika
- 1 1/2 tsp chili powder
- 1/4 cup mayonnaise
- 4 oz cream cheese
- 1 cup of water
- Pepper
- Salt

Directions:
1. Pour water into the instant pot then place the trivet in the pot.
2. Place corn on top of the trivet.
3. Seal pot with lid and cook on high for 5 minutes.
4. Once done, release pressure using quick release. Remove lid.
5. Remove corn and drain water from instant pot and clean the pot.
6. Cut corn from the cob. Add corn kernels, cayenne, cumin, garlic, paprika, chili powder, mayonnaise, cream cheese, pepper, and salt into the instant pot and stir well.
7. Seal pot with lid and cook on high for 5 minutes.
8. Once done, release pressure using quick release. Remove lid.
9. Add basil, cilantro, and lime juice and stir well.
10. Serve and enjoy.

Nutritional Value (Amount per Serving):
- Calories 199
- Fat 11.3 g
- Carbohydrates 23.7 g
- Sugar 4.3 g
- Protein 5.1 g
- Cholesterol 23 mg

Spicy Pepper Eggplant Spread

Preparation Time: 10 minutes
Cooking Time: 9 minutes
Serve: 4

Ingredients:

- 3 cups Italian eggplants, cut into 1/-inch chunks
- 1/2 cup tomatoes, diced
- 1 cup red pepper, diced
- 1/2 tsp red pepper flakes
- 1 tbsp vinegar
- 2 tbsp garlic, minced
- 1/2 cup onion, diced
- 2 tbsp olive oil
- 1/4 cup water
- 1 tsp kosher salt

Directions:

1. Add oil into the inner pot of instant pot and set the pot on sauté mode.
2. Add red pepper and eggplant and sauté for 5 minutes.
3. Add remaining ingredients and stir everything well.
4. Seal pot with lid and cook on high for 4 minutes.
5. Once done, release pressure using quick release. Remove lid.
6. Mash the spread mixture using the spatula and serve.

Nutritional Value (Amount per Serving):

- Calories 237
- Fat 19.2 g
- Carbohydrates 18 g
- Sugar 2.8 g
- Protein 1 g
- Cholesterol 0 mg

Chocolate Hummus

Preparation Time: 10 minutes
Cooking Time: 25 minutes
Serve: 10

Ingredients:
- 3/4 cup dried chickpeas, soaked overnight and drained
- 1 tsp vanilla
- 1/2 cup unsweetened cocoa powder
- 1/4 cup maple syrup
- 1/4 cup peanut butter
- 2 1/2 cups water
- Pinch of salt

Directions:
1. Add water and chickpeas into the instant pot.
2. Seal pot with lid and cook on high for 25 minutes.
3. Once done, release pressure using quick release. Remove lid.
4. Drain chickpeas well and reserved half cup of chickpea liquid.
5. Transfer chickpeas, reserved liquid, and remaining ingredients into the food processor and process until smooth.
6. Serve and enjoy.

Nutritional Value (Amount per Serving):
- Calories 124
- Fat 4.8 g
- Carbohydrates 18 g
- Sugar 7 g
- Protein 5.4 g
- Cholesterol 0 mg

Flavorful Roasted Baby Potatoes

Preparation Time: 10 minutes
Cooking Time: 10 minutes
Serve: 4

Ingredients:

- 2 lbs baby potatoes, clean and cut in half
- 1/2 cup vegetable stock
- 1 tsp paprika
- 3/4 tsp garlic powder
- 1 tsp onion powder
- 2 tsp Italian seasoning
- 1 tbsp olive oil
- Pepper
- Salt

Directions:

1. Add oil into the inner pot of instant pot and set the pot on sauté mode.
2. Add potatoes and sauté for 5 minutes. Add remaining ingredients and stir well.
3. Seal pot with lid and cook on high for 5 minutes.
4. Once done, release pressure using quick release. Remove lid.
5. Stir well and serve.

Nutritional Value (Amount per Serving):

- Calories 175
- Fat 4.5 g
- Carbohydrates 29.8 g
- Sugar 0.7 g
- Protein 6.1 g
- Cholesterol 2 mg

Slow Cooked Cheesy Artichoke Dip

Preparation Time: 10 minutes
Cooking Time: 60 minutes
Serve: 6

Ingredients:
- 10 oz can artichoke hearts, drained and chopped
- 4 cups spinach, chopped
- 8 oz cream cheese
- 3 tbsp sour cream
- 1/4 cup mayonnaise
- 3/4 cup mozzarella cheese, shredded
- 1/4 cup parmesan cheese, grated
- 3 garlic cloves, minced
- 1/2 tsp dried parsley
- Pepper
- Salt

Directions:
1. Add all ingredients into the inner pot of instant pot and stir well.
2. Seal the pot with the lid and select slow cook mode and set the timer for 60 minutes. Stir once while cooking.
3. Serve and enjoy.

Nutritional Value (Amount per Serving):
- Calories 226
- Fat 19.3 g
- Carbohydrates 7.5 g
- Sugar 1.2 g
- Protein 6.8 g
- Cholesterol 51 mg

Easy Tomato Dip

Preparation Time: 10 minutes
Cooking Time: 13 minutes
Serve: 4

Ingredients:
- 2 cups tomato puree
- 1/2 tsp ground cumin
- 1 tsp garlic, minced
- 1/4 cup vinegar
- 1 onion, chopped
- 1 tbsp olive oil
- Pepper
- Salt

Directions:
1. Add oil into the inner pot of instant pot and set the pot on sauté mode.
2. Add onion and sauté for 3 minutes.
3. Add remaining ingredients and stir well.
4. Seal pot with lid and cook on high for 10 minutes.
5. Once done, allow to release pressure naturally for 10 minutes then release remaining using quick release. Remove lid.
6. Blend tomato mixture using an immersion blender until smooth.
7. Serve and enjoy.

Nutritional Value (Amount per Serving):
- Calories 94
- Fat 3.9 g
- Carbohydrates 14.3 g
- Sugar 7.3 g
- Protein 2.5 g
- Cholesterol 0 mg

Spicy Chicken Dip

Preparation Time: 10 minutes
Cooking Time: 15 minutes
Serve: 10

Ingredients:

- 1 lb chicken breast, skinless and boneless
- 1/2 cup sour cream
- 8 oz cheddar cheese, shredded
- 1/2 cup chicken stock
- 2 jalapeno pepper, sliced
- 8 oz cream cheese
- Pepper
- Salt

Directions:

1. Add chicken, stock, jalapenos, and cream cheese into the instant pot.
2. Seal pot with lid and cook on high for 12 minutes.
3. Once done, release pressure using quick release. Remove lid.
4. Shred chicken using a fork.
5. Set pot on sauté mode. Add remaining ingredients and stir well and cook until cheese is melted.
6. Serve and enjoy.

Nutritional Value (Amount per Serving):

- Calories 248
- Fat 19 g
- Carbohydrates 1.6 g
- Sugar 0.3 g
- Protein 17.4 g
- Cholesterol 83 mg

Pinto Bean Dip

Preparation Time: 10 minutes
Cooking Time: 45 minutes
Serve: 6

Ingredients:
- 1 cup dry pinto beans
- 2 tsp chili powder
- 3 chilies de Arbol, remove the stem
- 4 cups of water
- 1 tsp salt

Directions:
1. Add beans, chilies, and water into the instant pot and stir well.
2. Seal pot with lid and cook on high for 45 minutes.
3. Once done, allow to release pressure naturally for 10 minutes then release remaining using quick release. Remove lid.
4. Transfer instant pot bean mixture into the blender along with chili powder and salt and blend until smooth.
5. Serve and enjoy.

Nutritional Value (Amount per Serving):
- Calories 139
- Fat 0.6 g
- Carbohydrates 24.6 g
- Sugar 4.2 g
- Protein 8 g
- Cholesterol 0 mg

Pepper Tomato Eggplant Spread

Preparation Time: 10 minutes
Cooking Time: 10 minutes
Serve: 3

Ingredients:
- 2 cups eggplant, chopped
- 1/4 cup vegetable broth
- 2 tbsp tomato paste
- 1/4 cup sun-dried tomatoes, minced
- 1 cup bell pepper, chopped
- 1 tsp garlic, minced
- 1 cup onion, chopped
- 3 tbsp olive oil
- Salt

Directions:
1. Add oil into the inner pot of instant pot and set the pot on sauté mode.
2. Add onion and sauté for 3 minutes.
3. Add eggplant, bell pepper, and garlic and sauté for 2 minutes.
4. Add remaining ingredients and stir well.
5. Seal pot with lid and cook on high for 5 minutes.
6. Once done, release pressure using quick release. Remove lid.
7. Lightly mash the eggplant mixture using a potato masher.
8. Stir well and serve.

Nutritional Value (Amount per Serving):
- Calories 178
- Fat 14.4 g
- Carbohydrates 12.8 g
- Sugar 7 g
- Protein 2.4 g
- Cholesterol 0 mg

Chapter 8: Poultry

Flavorful Cafe Rio Chicken

Preparation Time: 10 minutes
Cooking Time: 12 minutes
Serve: 6

Ingredients:

- 2 lbs chicken breasts, skinless and boneless
- 1/2 cup chicken stock
- 2 1/2 tbsp ranch seasoning
- 1/2 tbsp ground cumin
- 1/2 tbsp chili powder
- 1/2 tbsp garlic, minced
- 2/3 cup Italian dressing
- Pepper
- Salt

Directions:

1. Add chicken into the instant pot.
2. Mix together remaining ingredients and pour over chicken.
3. Seal pot with a lid and select manual and set timer for 12 minutes.
4. Once done, allow to release pressure naturally for 10 minutes then release remaining using quick release. Remove lid.
5. Shred the chicken using a fork and serve.

Nutritional Value (Amount per Serving):

- Calories 382
- Fat 18.9 g
- Carbohydrates 3.6 g
- Sugar 2.3 g
- Protein 44.1 g
- Cholesterol 152 mg

One Pot Chicken & Potatoes

Preparation Time: 10 minutes
Cooking Time: 13 minutes
Serve: 6

Ingredients:

- 6 chicken thighs, bone-in, and skin-on
- 1 tsp oregano
- 1 lb potatoes, halved
- 2 tbsp honey
- 1 fresh lemon juice
- 1 tsp garlic, minced
- 1 cup chicken stock
- 1 tsp paprika
- 1/2 tsp allspice
- 2 tbsp olive oil
- Pepper
- Salt

Directions:

1. In a small bowl, mix together 1 tablespoon oil, allspice, paprika, pepper, and salt and rub over chicken.
2. Add remaining oil into the instant pot and set the pot on sauté mode.
3. Add chicken to the pot and sauté until brown, about 5 minutes.
4. Add remaining ingredients and stir everything well.
5. Seal pot with lid and cook on high for 8 minutes.
6. Once done, allow to release pressure naturally for 5 minutes then release remaining using quick release. Remove lid.
7. Stir well and serve.

Nutritional Value (Amount per Serving):

- Calories 397
- Fat 15.8 g
- Carbohydrates 18.6 g
- Sugar 7 g
- Protein 43.8 g
- Cholesterol 130 mg

Flavorful Mediterranean Chicken

Preparation Time: 10 minutes
Cooking Time: 20 minutes
Serve: 8

Ingredients:

- 2 lbs chicken thighs
- 1/2 cup olives
- 28 oz can tomato, diced
- 1 1/2 tsp dried oregano
- 2 tsp dried parsley
- 1/2 tsp ground coriander powder
- 1/4 tsp chili pepper
- 1 tsp onion powder
- 1 sp paprika
- 2 cups onion, chopped
- 2 tbsp olive oil
- Pepper
- Salt

Directions:

1. Add oil into the inner pot of instant pot and set the pot on sauté mode.
2. Add chicken and cook until browned. Transfer chicken on a plate.
3. Add onion and sauté for 5 minutes.
4. Add all spices, tomatoes, and salt and cook for 2-3 minutes.
5. Return chicken to the pot and stir everything well.
6. Seal pot with lid and cook on high for 8 minutes.
7. Once done, release pressure using quick release. Remove lid.
8. Add olives and stir well.
9. Serve and enjoy.

Nutritional Value (Amount per Serving):

- Calories 292
- Fat 13 g
- Carbohydrates 8.9 g
- Sugar 4.8 g
- Protein 34.3 g
- Cholesterol 101 mg

Cheese Garlic Chicken & Potatoes

Preparation Time: 10 minutes
Cooking Time: 13 minutes
Serve: 4

Ingredients:
- 2 lbs chicken breasts, skinless, boneless, cut into chunks
- 1 tbsp olive oil
- 3/4 cup chicken broth
- 1 tbsp Italian seasoning
- 1 tbsp garlic powder
- 1 tsp garlic, minced
- 1 1/2 cup parmesan cheese, shredded
- 1 lb potatoes, chopped
- Pepper
- Salt

Directions:
1. Add oil into the inner pot of instant pot and set the pot on sauté mode.
2. Add chicken and cook until browned.
3. Add remaining ingredients except for cheese and stir well.
4. Seal pot with lid and cook on high for 8 minutes.
5. Once done, release pressure using quick release. Remove lid.
6. Top with cheese and cover with lid for 5 minutes or until cheese is melted.
7. Serve and enjoy.

Nutritional Value (Amount per Serving):
- Calories 674
- Fat 29 g
- Carbohydrates 21.4 g
- Sugar 2.3 g
- Protein 79.7 g
- Cholesterol 228 mg

Tasty Turkey Chili

Preparation Time: 10 minutes
Cooking Time: 25 minutes
Serve: 4

Ingredients:

- 1 lb cooked turkey, shredded
- 2 cups chicken broth
- 1 tsp tomato paste
- 1 small onion, chopped
- 1 tbsp Italian seasoning
- 1 tsp garlic powder
- 1 tbsp cumin, roasted
- 1 tbsp chili powder
- 2 cups tomatoes, crushed
- 1 tsp garlic, minced
- 14 oz can red beans, drained
- 14 oz can chickpeas, drained
- 1/2 cup corn
- 2 carrots, peeled and chopped
- 1/2 cup celery, chopped
- 1/4 cup edamame
- 2 tbsp olive oil
- Pepper
- Salt

Directions:

1. Add all ingredients into the instant pot and stir everything well.
2. Seal pot with lid and cook on high for 15 minutes.
3. Once done, allow to release pressure naturally. Remove lid.
4. Set pot on sauté mode and cook for 5-10 minutes or until chili thicken.
5. Stir well and serve.

Nutritional Value (Amount per Serving):

- Calories 593
- Fat 18.1 g
- Carbohydrates 56 g
- Sugar 7.3 g
- Protein 50.9 g
- Cholesterol 88 mg

Easy Chicken Scampi

Preparation Time: 10 minutes
Cooking Time: 25 minutes
Serve: 4

Ingredients:

- 3 chicken breasts, skinless, boneless, and sliced
- 1 tsp garlic, minced
- 1 tbsp Italian seasoning
- 2 cups chicken broth
- 1 bell pepper, sliced
- 1/2 onion, sliced
- Pepper
- Salt

Directions:

1. Add chicken into the instant pot and top with remaining ingredients.
2. Seal pot with lid and cook on high for 25 minutes.
3. Once done, release pressure using quick release. Remove lid.
4. Remove chicken from pot and shred using a fork. Return shredded chicken to the pot and stir well.
5. Serve over cooked whole grain pasta and top with cheese.

Nutritional Value (Amount per Serving):

- Calories 254
- Fat 9.9 g
- Carbohydrates 4.6 g
- Sugar 2.8 g
- Protein 34.6 g
- Cholesterol 100 mg

Lemon Olive Chicken

Preparation Time: 10 minutes
Cooking Time: 11 minutes
Serve: 8

Ingredients:

- 2 lbs chicken breasts, skinless and boneless
- 4 oz olives, pitted
- 2 lemons, quartered and remove seeds
- 1 cinnamon stick
- 1 tsp turmeric powder
- 1 tsp ground coriander
- 1 tsp ground ginger
- 1 tsp ground cumin
- 1 1/2 tsp paprika
- 1/2 cup chicken broth
- 1 tbsp garlic, minced
- 1 tbsp olive oil
- 2 onions, sliced
- Pepper
- Salt

Directions:

1. Add chicken, lemon, cinnamon, turmeric, coriander, ginger, cumin, paprika, pepper, and salt into the zip-lock bag. Seal bag shake well and place in refrigerator overnight.
2. Add oil into the inner pot of instant pot and set the pot on sauté mode.
3. Add garlic and onion and sauté for 5 minutes.
4. Add marinated chicken, broth, and olives and stir well.
5. Seal pot with lid and cook on high for 6 minutes.
6. Once done, allow to release pressure naturally for 10 minutes then release remaining using quick release. Remove lid.
7. Stir and serve.

Nutritional Value (Amount per Serving):

- Calories 271
- Fat 12 g
- Carbohydrates 6.1 g
- Sugar 1.7 g
- Protein 33.9 g
- Cholesterol 101 mg

Easy Chicken Piccata

Preparation Time: 10 minutes
Cooking Time: 41 minutes
Serve: 6

Ingredients:
- 8 chicken thighs, bone-in, and skin-on
- 2 tbsp fresh parsley, chopped
- 1 tbsp olive oil
- 3 tbsp capers
- 2 tbsp fresh lemon juice
- 1/2 cup chicken broth
- 1/4 cup dry white wine
- 1 tbsp garlic, minced

Directions:
1. Add oil into the inner pot of instant pot and set the pot on sauté mode.
2. Add garlic and sauté for 1 minute.
3. Add wine and cook for 5 minutes or until wine reduced by half.
4. Add lemon juice and broth and stir well.
5. Add chicken and seal pot with the lid and select manual and set a timer for 30 minutes.
6. Once done, release pressure using quick release. Remove lid.
7. Remove chicken from pot and place on a baking tray. Broil chicken for 5 minutes.
8. Add capers and stir well.
9. Garnish with parsley and serve.

Nutritional Value (Amount per Serving):
- Calories 406
- Fat 17 g
- Carbohydrates 1.2 g
- Sugar 0.3 g
- Protein 57 g
- Cholesterol 173 mg

Moroccan Spiced Chicken

Preparation Time: 10 minutes
Cooking Time: 20 minutes
Serve: 4

Ingredients:

- 1 lb chicken thighs, boneless and cut into chunks
- 1 cup can tomato, crushed
- 1/2 tsp red pepper flakes
- 1 tsp dried parsley
- 1/2 tsp coriander
- 1 tsp cumin
- 14 oz can chickpeas, drained and rinsed
- 2 tomatoes, chopped
- 1 tbsp garlic, minced
- 1 onion, sliced
- 2 red peppers, diced
- 1 tbsp olive oil
- Pepper
- Salt

Directions:

1. Add oil into the inner pot of instant pot and set the pot on sauté mode.
2. Add onion and garlic and sauté for 5 minutes.
3. Add chicken and cook for 5 minutes.
4. Add remaining ingredients and stir well.
5. Seal pot with lid and cook on high for 10 minutes.
6. Once done, release pressure using quick release. Remove lid.
7. Stir well and serve.

Nutritional Value (Amount per Serving):

- Calories 416
- Fat 21.3 g
- Carbohydrates 32.3 g
- Sugar 4 g
- Protein 26.1 g
- Cholesterol 96 mg

Shredded Greek Chicken

Preparation Time: 10 minutes
Cooking Time: 9 minutes
Serve: 4

Ingredients:
- 1 1/2 lbs chicken breasts, skinless and boneless
- 12 oz jar marinated artichoke hearts, drained and chopped
- 12 oz jar roasted red peppers, drained and chopped
- 1 cup chicken broth
- 1/2 lemon juice
- 1/2 tsp dill
- 1/2 tbsp basil
- 1 tbsp oregano
- 1 tbsp garlic, minced
- 1 onion, diced
- 1 tbsp olive oil
- Pepper
- Salt

Directions:
1. Add oil into the inner pot of instant pot and set the pot on sauté mode.
2. Add garlic and onion and sauté for 2-3 minutes.
3. Add chicken, lemon juice, broth, and all seasonings. Stir well.
4. Seal pot with lid and cook on high for 6 minutes.
5. Once done, allow to release pressure naturally for 5 minutes then release remaining using quick release. Remove lid.
6. Remove chicken from pot and shred using a fork.
7. Return shredded chicken to the pot along with roasted peppers and artichoke and stir well.
8. Serve over rice.

Nutritional Value (Amount per Serving):
- Calories 543
- Fat 29.5 g
- Carbohydrates 14.7 g
- Sugar 5.4 g
- Protein 53.4 g
- Cholesterol 151 mg

Delicious Gyro Chicken

Preparation Time: 10 minutes
Cooking Time: 12 minutes
Serve: 3

Ingredients:

- 1 lb chicken thighs
- 1 cup chicken broth
- 1 tsp garlic, minced
- 1 tbsp fresh lemon juice
- 1 tbsp olive oil
- 2 tbsp fresh cilantro, chopped
- 1 tbsp green onion, chopped
- 1/2 tsp oregano
- 1/2 tsp cumin powder
- 1/2 tsp ground cinnamon
- 1/2 tsp paprika
- 1/2 tsp Adobo seasoning
- 1 onion, sliced
- Pepper
- Salt

Directions:

1. Season chicken with oregano, cinnamon, cumin, paprika, adobo seasoning, pepper, and salt and place into the instant pot.
2. Pour remaining ingredients over chicken.
3. Seal pot with lid and cook on high for 12 minutes.
4. Once done, release pressure using quick release. Remove lid.
5. Stir well and serve.

Nutritional Value (Amount per Serving):

- Calories 362
- Fat 16.6 g
- Carbohydrates 5.2 g
- Sugar 2 g
- Protein 46.1 g
- Cholesterol 135 mg

Chapter 9: Beef

Flavorful Beef Bourguignon

Preparation Time: 10 minutes
Cooking Time: 20 minutes
Serve: 4

Ingredients:
- 1 1/2 lbs beef chuck roast, cut into chunks
- 2/3 cup beef stock
- 2 tbsp fresh thyme
- 1 bay leaf
- 1 tsp garlic, minced
- 8 oz mushrooms, sliced
- 2 tbsp tomato paste
- 2/3 cup dry red wine
- 1 onion, sliced
- 4 carrots, cut into chunks
- 1 tbsp olive oil
- Pepper
- Salt

Directions:
1. Add oil into the instant pot and set the pot on sauté mode.
2. Add meat and sauté until brown. Add onion and sauté until softened.
3. Add remaining ingredients and stir well.
4. Seal pot with lid and cook on high for 12 minutes.
5. Once done, allow to release pressure naturally. Remove lid.
6. Stir well and serve.

Nutritional Value (Amount per Serving):
- Calories 744
- Fat 51.3 g
- Carbohydrates 14.5 g
- Sugar 6.5 g
- Protein 48.1 g
- Cholesterol 175 mg

Cauliflower Tomato Beef

Preparation Time: 10 minutes
Cooking Time: 25 minutes
Serve: 2

Ingredients:

- 1/2 lb beef stew meat, chopped
- 1 tsp paprika
- 1 tbsp balsamic vinegar
- 1 celery stalk, chopped
- 1/4 cup grape tomatoes, chopped
- 1 onion, chopped
- 1 tbsp olive oil
- 1/4 cup cauliflower, chopped
- Pepper
- Salt

Directions:

1. Add oil into the instant pot and set the pot on sauté mode.
2. Add meat and sauté for 5 minutes.
3. Add remaining ingredients and stir well.
4. Seal pot with lid and cook on high for 20 minutes.
5. Once done, allow to release pressure naturally. Remove lid.
6. Stir and serve.

Nutritional Value (Amount per Serving):

- Calories 306
- Fat 14.3 g
- Carbohydrates 7.6 g
- Sugar 3.5 g
- Protein 35.7 g
- Cholesterol 101 mg

Delicious Beef Chili

Preparation Time: 10 minutes
Cooking Time: 35 minutes
Serve: 8

Ingredients:
- 2 lbs ground beef
- 1 tsp olive oil
- 1 tsp garlic, minced
- 1 small onion, chopped
- 2 tbsp chili powder
- 1 tsp oregano
- 1/2 tsp thyme
- 28 oz can tomatoes, crushed
- 2 cups beef stock
- 2 carrots, chopped
- 3 sweet potatoes, peeled and cubed
- Pepper
- Salt

Directions:
1. Add oil into the instant pot and set the pot on sauté mode.
2. Add meat and cook until brown.
3. Add remaining ingredients and stir well.
4. Seal pot with lid and cook on high for 35 minutes.
5. Once done, allow to release pressure naturally. Remove lid.
6. Stir well and serve.

Nutritional Value (Amount per Serving):
- Calories 302
- Fat 8.2 g
- Carbohydrates 19.2 g
- Sugar 4.8 g
- Protein 37.1 g
- Cholesterol 101 mg

Moist Shredded Beef

Preparation Time: 10 minutes
Cooking Time: 20 minutes
Serve: 8

Ingredients:

- 2 lbs beef chuck roast, cut into chunks
- 1/2 tbsp dried red pepper
- 1 tbsp Italian seasoning
- 1 tbsp garlic, minced
- 2 tbsp vinegar
- 14 oz can fire-roasted tomatoes
- 1/2 cup bell pepper, chopped
- 1/2 cup carrots, chopped
- 1 cup onion, chopped
- 1 tsp salt

Directions:

1. Add all ingredients into the inner pot of instant pot and set the pot on sauté mode.
2. Seal pot with lid and cook on high for 20 minutes.
3. Once done, release pressure using quick release. Remove lid.
4. Shred the meat using a fork.
5. Stir well and serve.

Nutritional Value (Amount per Serving):

- Calories 456
- Fat 32.7 g
- Carbohydrates 7.7 g
- Sugar 4.1 g
- Protein 31 g
- Cholesterol 118 mg

Beef Curry

Preparation Time: 10 minutes
Cooking Time: 30 minutes
Serve: 2

Ingredients:
- 1/2 lb beef stew meat, cubed
- 1 bell peppers, sliced
- 1 cup beef stock
- 1 tbsp fresh ginger, grated
- 1/2 tsp ground cumin
- 1 tsp ground coriander
- 1/2 tsp cayenne pepper
- 1/2 cup sun-roasted tomatoes, diced
- 2 tbsp olive oil
- 1 tsp garlic, crushed
- 1 green chili peppers, chopped

Directions:
1. Add all ingredients into the instant pot and stir well.
2. Seal pot with lid and cook on high for 30 minutes.
3. Once done, allow to release pressure naturally. Remove lid.
4. Serve and enjoy.

Nutritional Value (Amount per Serving):
- Calories 391
- Fat 21.9 g
- Carbohydrates 11.6 g
- Sugar 5.8 g
- Protein 37.4 g
- Cholesterol 101 mg

Delicious Ground Beef

Preparation Time: 10 minutes
Cooking Time: 10 minutes
Serve: 4

Ingredients:

- 1 lb ground beef
- 1 tbsp olive oil
- 2 tbsp tomato paste
- 1 cup chicken broth
- 12 oz cheddar cheese, shredded
- 1 tbsp Italian seasoning
- Pepper
- Salt

Directions:

1. Add oil into the instant pot and set the pot on sauté mode.
2. Add meat and cook until browned.
3. Add remaining ingredients except for cheese and stir well.
4. Seal pot with lid and cook on high for 7 minutes.
5. Once done, release pressure using quick release. Remove lid.
6. Add cheese and stir well and cook on sauté mode until cheese is melted.
7. Serve and enjoy.

Nutritional Value (Amount per Serving):

- Calories 610
- Fat 40.2 g
- Carbohydrates 3.2 g
- Sugar 1.9 g
- Protein 57.2 g
- Cholesterol 193 mg

Hearty Beef Ragu

Preparation Time: 10 minutes
Cooking Time: 50 minutes
Serve: 4

Ingredients:
- 1 1/2 lbs beef steak, diced
- 1 1/2 cup beef stock
- 1 tbsp coconut amino
- 14 oz can tomatoes, chopped
- 1/2 tsp ground cinnamon
- 1 tsp dried oregano
- 1 tsp dried thyme
- 1 tsp dried basil
- 1 tsp paprika
- 1 bay leaf
- 1 tbsp garlic, chopped
- 1/2 tsp cayenne pepper
- 1 celery stick, diced
- 1 carrot, diced
- 1 onion, diced
- 2 tbsp olive oil
- 1/4 tsp pepper
- 1 1/2 tsp sea salt

Directions:
1. Add oil into the instant pot and set the pot on sauté mode.
2. Add celery, carrots, onion, and salt and sauté for 5 minutes.
3. Add meat and remaining ingredients and stir everything well.
4. Seal pot with lid and cook on high for 30 minutes.
5. Once done, allow to release pressure naturally for 10 minutes then release remaining using quick release. Remove lid.
6. Shred meat using a fork. Set pot on sauté mode and cook for 10 minutes. Stir every 2-3 minutes.
7. Serve and enjoy.

Nutritional Value (Amount per Serving):
- Calories 435
- Fat 18.1 g
- Carbohydrates 12.3 g
- Sugar 5.5 g
- Protein 54.4 g
- Cholesterol 152 mg

Sage Tomato Beef

Preparation Time: 10 minutes
Cooking Time: 40 minutes
Serve: 4

Ingredients:
- 2 lbs beef stew meat, cubed
- 1/4 cup tomato paste
- 1 tsp garlic, minced
- 2 cups chicken stock
- 1 onion, chopped
- 2 tbsp olive oil
- 1 tbsp sage, chopped
- Pepper
- Salt

Directions:
1. Add oil into the instant pot and set the pot on sauté mode.
2. Add garlic and onion and sauté for 5 minutes.
3. Add meat and sauté for 5 minutes.
4. Add remaining ingredients and stir well.
5. Seal pot with lid and cook on high for 30 minutes.
6. Once done, allow to release pressure naturally. Remove lid.
7. Serve and enjoy.

Nutritional Value (Amount per Serving):
- Calories 515
- Fat 21.5 g
- Carbohydrates 7 g
- Sugar 3.6 g
- Protein 70 g
- Cholesterol 203 mg

Beef Shawarma

Preparation Time: 10 minutes
Cooking Time: 10 minutes
Serve: 2

Ingredients:
- 1/2 lb ground beef
- 1/4 tsp cinnamon
- 1/2 tsp dried oregano
- 1 cup cabbage, cut into strips
- 1/2 cup bell pepper, sliced
- 1/4 tsp ground coriander
- 1/4 tsp cumin
- 1/4 tsp cayenne pepper
- 1/4 tsp ground allspice
- 1/2 cup onion, chopped
- 1/2 tsp salt

Directions:
1. Set instant pot on sauté mode.
2. Add meat to the pot and sauté until brown.
3. Add remaining ingredients and stir well.
4. Seal pot with lid and cook on high for 5 minutes.
5. Once done, release pressure using quick release. Remove lid.
6. Stir and serve.

Nutritional Value (Amount per Serving):
- Calories 245
- Fat 7.4 g
- Carbohydrates 7.9 g
- Sugar 3.9 g
- Protein 35.6 g
- Cholesterol 101 mg

Rosemary Beef Eggplant

Preparation Time: 10 minutes
Cooking Time: 30 minutes
Serve: 4

Ingredients:
- 1 lb beef stew meat, cubed
- 2 tbsp green onion, chopped
- 1/4 tsp red pepper flakes
- 1/2 tsp dried rosemary
- 1/2 tsp paprika
- 1 cup chicken stock
- 1 onion, chopped
- 1 eggplant, cubed
- 2 tbsp olive oil
- Pepper
- Salt

Directions:
1. Add oil into the instant pot and set the pot on sauté mode.
2. Add meat and onion and sauté for 5 minutes.
3. Add remaining ingredients and stir well.
4. Seal pot with lid and cook on high for 25 minutes.
5. Once done, allow to release pressure naturally. Remove lid.
6. Serve and enjoy.

Nutritional Value (Amount per Serving):
- Calories 315
- Fat 14.5 g
- Carbohydrates 10 g
- Sugar 4.9 g
- Protein 36.1 g
- Cholesterol 101 mg

Lemon Basil Beef

Preparation Time: 10 minutes
Cooking Time: 35 minutes
Serve: 4

Ingredients:

- 1 1/2 lb beef stew meat, cut into cubes
- 1/2 cup fresh basil, chopped
- 1/2 tsp dried thyme
- 2 cups chicken stock
- 1 tsp garlic, minced
- 2 tbsp lemon juice
- 1 onion, chopped
- 2 tbsp olive oil
- Pepper
- Salt

Directions:

1. Add oil into the instant pot and set the pot on sauté mode.
2. Add meat, garlic, and onion and sauté for 5 minutes.
3. Add remaining ingredients and stir well.
4. Seal pot with lid and cook on high for 30 minutes.
5. Once done, allow to release pressure naturally. Remove lid.
6. Serve and enjoy.

Nutritional Value (Amount per Serving):

- Calories 396
- Fat 18 g
- Carbohydrates 3.5 g
- Sugar 1.7 g
- Protein 52.4 g
- Cholesterol 152 mg

Chapter 10: Pork

Walnut Pork Chops

Preparation Time: 10 minutes
Cooking Time: 30 minutes
Serve: 4

Ingredients:

- 4 pork chops
- 1 cup chicken stock
- 2 red chili, chopped
- 2 tbsp walnuts, chopped
- 1 tbsp garlic, minced
- 1 small onion, chopped
- 1 tbsp olive oil
- Pepper
- Salt

Directions:

1. Add oil into the inner pot of instant pot and set the pot on sauté mode.
2. Add garlic and onion and sauté for 5 minutes.
3. Add pork chops and cook for 5 minutes.
4. Add remaining ingredients and stir well.
5. Seal pot with lid and cook on high for 20 minutes.
6. Once done, allow to release pressure naturally for 10 minutes then release remaining using quick release. Remove lid.
7. Serve and enjoy.

Nutritional Value (Amount per Serving):

- Calories 324
- Fat 25.9 g
- Carbohydrates 3.1 g
- Sugar 1.1 g
- Protein 19.4 g
- Cholesterol 69 mg

Lime Salsa Pork Chops

Preparation Time: 10 minutes
Cooking Time: 25 minutes
Serve: 4

Ingredients:
- 1 1/2 lbs pork chops
- 1/2 tsp garlic powder
- 1/2 tsp ground cumin
- 2 tbsp lime juice
- 1/2 cup salsa
- 1 tbsp olive oil
- Pepper
- Salt

Directions:
1. Add oil into the inner pot of instant pot and set the pot on sauté mode.
2. Add pork chops and sauté until brown.
3. Add remaining ingredients and stir well.
4. Seal pot with lid and cook on high for 15 minutes.
5. Once done, release pressure using quick release. Remove lid.
6. Serve and enjoy.

Nutritional Value (Amount per Serving):
- Calories 591
- Fat 45.9 g
- Carbohydrates 4.3 g
- Sugar 1.5 g
- Protein 38.9 g
- Cholesterol 146 mg

Pork Roast with Potatoes

Preparation Time: 10 minutes
Cooking Time: 30 minutes
Serve: 4

Ingredients:

- 2 lbs pork roast, sliced
- 1 tbsp fresh parsley, chopped
- 1 cup chicken stock
- 1 tbsp olive oil
- 1/2 tsp rosemary, chopped
- 1 tsp chili powder
- 1 cup heavy cream
- 1 onion, chopped
- 2 sweet potatoes, peeled and cubed
- Pepper
- Salt

Directions:

1. Add oil into the inner pot of instant pot and set the pot on sauté mode.
2. Add onion and meat and sauté for 5 minutes.
3. Add remaining ingredients except for heavy cream and stir well.
4. Seal pot with lid and cook on high for 25 minutes.
5. Once done, allow to release pressure naturally for 10 minutes then release remaining using quick release. Remove lid.
6. Stir in heavy cream and serve.

Nutritional Value (Amount per Serving):

- Calories 664
- Fat 36.4 g
- Carbohydrates 14.6 g
- Sugar 1.6 g
- Protein 66.4 g
- Cholesterol 236 mg

Pork with Vegetables

Preparation Time: 10 minutes
Cooking Time: 22 minutes
Serve: 4

Ingredients:

- 1 lb pork, cut into chunks
- 2 potatoes, quarters
- 1 lb green beans
- 3 tomatoes, chopped
- 2 celery sticks, sliced
- 2 carrots, sliced
- 1/2 cup olive oil
- 1 onion, chopped
- Pepper
- Salt

Directions:

1. Add oil into the inner pot of instant pot and set the pot on sauté mode.
2. Add meat and cook for 5 minutes.
3. Add remaining ingredients and stir everything well.
4. Seal pot with lid and cook on high for 17 minutes.
5. Once done, release pressure using quick release. Remove lid.
6. Stir well and serve.

Nutritional Value (Amount per Serving):

- Calories 527
- Fat 29.6 g
- Carbohydrates 34.1 g
- Sugar 7.9 g
- Protein 34.9 g
- Cholesterol 83 mg

Pork with Beans

Preparation Time: 10 minutes
Cooking Time: 35 minutes
Serve: 4

Ingredients:

- 2 lbs pork shoulder, boneless and cut into chunks
- 1 tsp ground cumin
- 1 cup chicken stock
- 1 cup green beans, cut into pieces
- 1/2 cup corn
- 1 tsp garlic, minced
- Pepper
- Salt

Directions:

1. Add all ingredients into the inner pot of instant pot and stir well.
2. Seal pot with lid and cook on high for 35 minutes.
3. Once done, allow to release pressure naturally. Remove lid.
4. Serve and enjoy.

Nutritional Value (Amount per Serving):

- Calories 693
- Fat 49 g
- Carbohydrates 6.3 g
- Sugar 1.2 g
- Protein 54.2 g
- Cholesterol 204 mg

Pork Rice

Preparation Time: 10 minutes
Cooking Time: 30 minutes
Serve: 2

Ingredients:

- 1 lb pork tenderloin, cut into 1-inch pieces
- 1/2 cup rice
- 7 oz can black beans, rinsed and drained
- 1 tsp garlic, chopped
- 1/4 cup orange juice
- 1 tbsp fresh cilantro, chopped
- 1/2 tbsp fresh lime juice
- 1 cup chicken broth
- 1 tbsp olive oil
- 1/2 tsp ground cumin
- Salt

Directions:

1. Add oil into the instant pot and set the pot on sauté mode.
2. Add meat to the pot and sauté for 5 minutes.
3. Stir in orange juice, cumin, garlic, broth, rice, and beans.
4. Seal pot with lid and cook on high for 12 minutes.
5. Once done, release pressure using quick release. Remove lid.
6. Stir in lime juice and garnish with cilantro.
7. Serve and enjoy.

Nutritional Value (Amount per Serving):

- Calories 685
- Fat 16.5 g
- Carbohydrates 59.8 g
- Sugar 4 g
- Protein 70.9 g
- Cholesterol 166 mg

Cheese Pork Chops

Preparation Time: 10 minutes
Cooking Time: 15 minutes
Serve: 2

Ingredients:

- 2 pork chops, boneless
- 1/2 tbsp olive oil
- 1/2 tbsp Italian seasoning
- 3 oz feta cheese, crumbled
- 3/4 cup chicken stock
- 1/2 tsp garlic powder
- Pepper
- Salt

Directions:

1. Season pork chops with Italian seasoning, garlic powder, pepper, and salt and set aside.
2. Add oil into the instant pot and set the pot on sauté mode.
3. Add pork chops and cook until brown. Pour stock over pork chops.
4. Seal pot with lid and cook on high for 10 minutes.
5. Once done, allow to release pressure naturally for 10 minutes then release remaining using quick release. Remove lid.
6. Top with cheese and serve.

Nutritional Value (Amount per Serving):

- Calories 415
- Fat 33.7 g
- Carbohydrates 2.9 g
- Sugar 2.5 g
- Protein 24.4 g
- Cholesterol 109 mg

Capers Pork Chops

Preparation Time: 10 minutes
Cooking Time: 25 minutes
Serve: 4

Ingredients:

- 4 pork chops
- 2 tbsp parsley, chopped
- 1/2 cup tomatoes, chopped
- 1 tsp paprika
- 1/2 tsp chili powder
- 1/2 tsp ground coriander
- 1 tbsp capers, chopped
- 1 tsp ground cumin
- 1 tbsp olive oil
- Pepper
- Salt

Directions:

1. Add oil into the inner pot of instant pot and set the pot on sauté mode.
2. Add pork chops and sauté for 5 minutes.
3. Add remaining ingredients stir well.
4. Seal pot with lid and cook on high for 20 minutes.
5. Once done, allow to release pressure naturally. Remove lid.
6. Serve and enjoy.

Nutritional Value (Amount per Serving):

- Calories 269
- Fat 23.7 g
- Carbohydrates 1.8 g
- Sugar 0.7 g
- Protein 18.5 g
- Cholesterol 69 mg

Garlic Parsley Pork Chops

Preparation Time: 10 minutes
Cooking Time: 25 minutes
Serve: 4

Ingredients:

- 4 pork chops, boneless
- 1 tbsp garlic, minced
- 1/2 cup tomato puree
- 1 cup chicken stock
- 1 onion, chopped
- 1 tbsp fresh parsley, chopped
- 1 tbsp olive oil
- Pepper
- Salt

Directions:

1. Add oil into the inner pot of instant pot and set the pot on sauté mode.
2. Add garlic and onion and sauté for 2 minutes.
3. Add pork chops and sauté for 3 minutes.
4. Add remaining ingredients and stir well.
5. Seal pot with lid and cook on high for 20 minutes.
6. Once done, allow to release pressure naturally for 10 minutes then release remaining using quick release. Remove lid.
7. Stir and serve.

Nutritional Value (Amount per Serving):

- Calories 315
- Fat 23.6 g
- Carbohydrates 6.3 g
- Sugar 2.9 g
- Protein 19.1 g
- Cholesterol 69 mg

Pork with Carrots Potatoes

Preparation Time: 10 minutes
Cooking Time: 15 minutes
Serve: 2

Ingredients:

- 2 pork chops, boneless
- 1/4 cup balsamic vinegar
- 2 tbsp honey
- 1 1/2 tsp ground ginger
- 1 tsp curry powder
- 1/2 cup chicken stock
- 1 tbsp olive oil
- 3 carrots, chopped
- 3 small potatoes, cubed
- 2 garlic cloves, chopped
- Pepper
- Salt

Directions:

1. Add oil into the instant pot and set the pot on sauté mode.
2. Add pork chops into the pot and brown them from both the sides.
3. Add remaining ingredients to the pot and stir well.
4. Seal pot with lid and cook on high for 10 minutes.
5. Once done, allow to release pressure naturally. Open the lid.
6. Serve and enjoy.

Nutritional Value (Amount per Serving):

- Calories 615
- Fat 27.5 g
- Carbohydrates 69.4 g
- Sugar 25.1 g
- Protein 23.7 g
- Cholesterol 69 mg

Simple Shredded Pork

Preparation Time: 10 minutes
Cooking Time: 35 minutes
Serve: 2

Ingredients:
- 1/2 lb pork belly, cut into cubes
- 1 tsp thyme
- 1/2 cup onion, chopped
- 1/2 cup chicken stock
- 1 1/2 tsp pepper
- 1/4 tsp salt

Directions:
1. Add all ingredients to the instant pot and stir well.
2. Seal pot with lid and cook on high for 35 minutes.
3. Once done, release pressure using quick release. Remove lid.
4. Remove meat from pot and shred using a fork.
5. Serve and enjoy.

Nutritional Value (Amount per Serving):
- Calories 543
- Fat 30.8 g
- Carbohydrates 4.2 g
- Sugar 1.4 g
- Protein 53.1 g
- Cholesterol 131 mg

Chapter 11: Lamb

Delicious Salsa Lamb

Preparation Time: 10 minutes
Cooking Time: 35 minutes
Serve: 4

Ingredients:
- 1 lb lamb shoulder, cut into chunks
- 1/4 cup fresh cilantro, chopped
- 2 tbsp olive oil
- 1 onion, chopped
- 1 tsp garlic, minced
- 1 1/2 cups salsa
- Pepper
- Salt

Directions:
1. Add oil into the inner pot of instant pot and set the pot on sauté mode.
2. Add garlic and onion and sauté for 5 minutes.
3. Add remaining ingredients and stir well.
4. Seal pot with lid and cook on high for 30 minutes.
5. Once done, allow to release pressure naturally. Remove lid.
6. Stir well and serve.

Nutritional Value (Amount per Serving):
- Calories 310
- Fat 15.5 g
- Carbohydrates 9 g
- Sugar 4.2 g
- Protein 33.7 g
- Cholesterol 102 mg

Sweet Potato lamb

Preparation Time: 10 minutes
Cooking Time: 35 minutes
Serve: 4

Ingredients:

- 1 lb lamb shoulder, cut into chunks
- 2 tbsp olive oil
- 1 cup beef stock
- 2 sweet potatoes, cubed
- 1 tsp garlic, minced
- 1 onion, chopped
- 1 carrot, chopped
- Pepper
- Salt

Directions:

1. Add oil into the inner pot of instant pot and set the pot on sauté mode.
2. Add garlic and onion and sauté for 2 minutes.
3. Add meat and sauté for 3 minutes.
4. Add remaining ingredients and stir well.
5. Seal pot with lid and cook on high for 30 minutes.
6. Once done, allow to release pressure naturally. Remove lid.
7. Stir well and serve.

Nutritional Value (Amount per Serving):

- Calories 338
- Fat 15.5 g
- Carbohydrates 14.8 g
- Sugar 2.1 g
- Protein 33.6 g
- Cholesterol 102 mg

Healthy Quinoa Lamb

Preparation Time: 10 minutes
Cooking Time: 25 minutes
Serve: 4

Ingredients:

- 1 lb lamb shoulder, cut into chunks
- 1 tbsp chives, chopped
- 1/4 cup can tomatoes, crushed
- 2 cups beef stock
- 1 onion, chopped
- 1 1/2 cups quinoa, rinsed and drained
- Pepper
- Salt

Directions:

1. Add all ingredients into the inner pot of instant pot and stir well.
2. Seal pot with lid and cook on high for 25 minutes.
3. Once done, allow to release pressure naturally for 10 minutes then release remaining using quick release. Remove lid.
4. Stir well and serve.

Nutritional Value (Amount per Serving):

- Calories 469
- Fat 12.5 g
- Carbohydrates 44.3 g
- Sugar 1.7 g
- Protein 42.7 g
- Cholesterol 102 mg

Tomato Oregano Lamb Stew

Preparation Time: 10 minutes
Cooking Time: 40 minutes
Serve: 4

Ingredients:

- 4 lamb shanks
- 2 cups beef stock
- 1 tbsp oregano, chopped
- 1 1/2 cups tomatoes, chopped
- 1 tsp garlic, minced
- 1 onion, chopped
- 2 tbsp olive oil
- Pepper
- Salt

Directions:

1. Add oil into the inner pot of instant pot and set the pot on sauté mode.
2. Add lamb and sear for 5 minutes.
3. Add the rest of the ingredients and stir well.
4. Seal pot with lid and cook on low pressure for 35 minutes.
5. Once done, allow to release pressure naturally. Remove lid.
6. Serve and enjoy.

Nutritional Value (Amount per Serving):

- Calories 704
- Fat 31.5 g
- Carbohydrates 6.2 g
- Sugar 3 g
- Protein 94.2 g
- Cholesterol 294 mg

Italian Lamb Stew

Preparation Time: 10 minutes
Cooking Time: 30 minutes
Serve: 4

Ingredients:

- 2 lbs lamb, cut into chunks
- 1/2 cup cilantro, chopped
- 1 tsp dried oregano
- 1 tbsp olive oil
- 1 cup tomatoes, chopped
- 1 cup olives, pitted and sliced
- 1 onion, chopped
- 1 tbsp garlic, minced
- Pepper
- Salt

Directions:

1. Add oil into the inner pot of instant pot and set the pot on sauté mode.
2. Add oregano, garlic, and onion and sauté for 5 minutes.
3. Add meat and sauté for 5 minutes.
4. Add the rest of the ingredients and stir well.
5. Seal pot with lid and cook on high for 20 minutes.
6. Once done, allow to release pressure naturally. Remove lid.
7. Serve and enjoy.

Nutritional Value (Amount per Serving):

- Calories 514
- Fat 23.9 g
- Carbohydrates 7.4 g
- Sugar 2.4 g
- Protein 64.9 g
- Cholesterol 204 mg

Lamb Stew

Preparation Time: 10 minutes
Cooking Time: 30 minutes
Serve: 4

Ingredients:

- 2 lbs lamb shoulder, cut into cubes
- 1 tsp dried basil
- 1 tsp dried oregano
- 1 tbsp olive oil
- 2 onion, chopped
- 14 oz can tomatoes, chopped
- 1 tbsp garlic, minced
- Pepper
- Salt

Directions:

1. Add oil into the inner pot of instant pot and set the pot on sauté mode.
2. Add meat, onion, and garlic and sauté for 5 minutes.
3. Add remaining ingredients and stir well.
4. Seal pot with lid and cook on high for 25 minutes.
5. Once done, allow to release pressure naturally for 10 minutes then release remaining using quick release. Remove lid.
6. Stir well and serve.

Nutritional Value (Amount per Serving):

- Calories 499
- Fat 20.2 g
- Carbohydrates 11.2 g
- Sugar 5.7 g
- Protein 65.4 g
- Cholesterol 204 mg

Tomato Lamb Chops

Preparation Time: 10 minutes
Cooking Time: 30 minutes
Serve: 4

Ingredients:
- 4 lamb chopped
- 1 cup chicken stock
- 1 tsp herb de province
- 1 tsp garlic, minced
- 2 cups can tomatoes, chopped
- Pepper
- Salt

Directions:
1. Add all ingredients into the inner pot of instant pot and stir well.
2. Seal pot with lid and cook on high for 30 minutes.
3. Once done, allow to release pressure naturally. Remove lid.
4. Stir well and serve.

Nutritional Value (Amount per Serving):
- Calories 375
- Fat 17.1 g
- Carbohydrates 6.4 g
- Sugar 4.2 g
- Protein 23 g
- Cholesterol 82 mg

Flavors Lamb Ribs

Preparation Time: 10 minutes
Cooking Time: 25 minutes
Serve: 4

Ingredients:
- 4 lamb ribs
- 2 tomatoes, chopped
- 2 tbsp olive oil
- 1 1/2 cups chicken stock
- 1 tbsp sage, chopped
- 1 tbsp garlic, minced
- Pepper
- Salt

Directions:
1. Add oil into the inner pot of instant pot and set the pot on sauté mode.
2. Add lamb ribs and sear for 5 minutes.
3. Add remaining ingredients except for heavy cream and stir well.
4. Seal pot with lid and cook on high for 20 minutes.
5. Once done, allow to release pressure naturally for 10 minutes then release remaining using quick release. Remove lid.
6. Serve and enjoy.

Nutritional Value (Amount per Serving):
- Calories 539
- Fat 46.1 g
- Carbohydrates 10.9 g
- Sugar 7.2 g
- Protein 22.6 g
- Cholesterol 0 mg

Mediterranean Lamb

Preparation Time: 10 minutes
Cooking Time: 35 minutes
Serve: 4

Ingredients:

- 2 1/2 lbs lamb shoulder, cut into chunks
- 1 bay leaf
- 1 cup vegetable stock
- 10 oz prunes, soaked
- 1 tsp garlic, minced
- 2 tbsp honey
- 2 onions, sliced
- 1 tsp ground cumin
- 1 tsp ground ginger
- 1 tsp ground turmeric
- 1/4 tsp cinnamon
- 3 oz almonds sliced
- Pepper
- Salt

Directions:

1. Add all ingredients into the inner pot of instant pot and stir well.
2. Seal pot with lid and cook on high for 35 minutes.
3. Once done, allow to release pressure naturally. Remove lid.
4. Serve and enjoy.

Nutritional Value (Amount per Serving):

- Calories 886
- Fat 32 g
- Carbohydrates 65.3 g
- Sugar 38.8 g
- Protein 86.5 g
- Cholesterol 255 mg

Curried Lamb Stew

Preparation Time: 10 minutes
Cooking Time: 20 minutes
Serve: 4

Ingredients:
- 1 lb lamb shoulder, cut into cubes
- 1/4 cup heavy cream
- 2 cups beef stock
- 1 tbsp basil, chopped
- 1 tsp chili powder
- 1/2 tbsp curry powder
- 1 onion, chopped
- 1 tbsp olive oil
- Pepper
- Salt

Directions:
1. Add oil into the inner pot of instant pot and set the pot on sauté mode.
2. Add onion and sauté for 5 minutes.
3. Add meat and sauté for 5 minutes.
4. Add the rest of ingredients except cream and stir well.
5. Seal pot with lid and cook on high for 10 minutes.
6. Once done, release pressure using quick release. Remove lid.
7. Stir in cream and serve.

Nutritional Value (Amount per Serving):
- Calories 291
- Fat 15.1 g
- Carbohydrates 3.7 g
- Sugar 1.3 g
- Protein 33.9 g
- Cholesterol 112 mg

Garlic Coriander Lamb Chops

Preparation Time: 10 minutes
Cooking Time: 30 minutes
Serve: 4

Ingredients:

- 4 lamb chops
- 1 tbsp cilantro, chopped
- 1 cup beef stock
- 1/2 tsp ground coriander
- 1 tsp chili powder
- 1 tsp turmeric powder
- 1 tbsp garlic, minced
- 2 tbsp olive oil
- Pepper
- Salt

Directions:

1. Add oil into the inner pot of instant pot and set the pot on sauté mode.
2. Add garlic, lamb chops, chili powder, and turmeric and sauté for 5 minutes.
3. Add the rest of the ingredients and stir well.
4. Seal pot with lid and cook on high for 25 minutes.
5. Once done, allow to release pressure naturally. Remove lid.
6. Serve and enjoy.

Nutritional Value (Amount per Serving):

- Calories 680
- Fat 31.3 g
- Carbohydrates 1.6 g
- Sugar 0.1 g
- Protein 92.8 g
- Cholesterol 294 mg

Chapter 12: Seafood & Fish

Pesto Fish Fillet

Preparation Time: 10 minutes
Cooking Time: 8 minutes
Serve: 4

Ingredients:

- 4 halibut fillets
- 1/2 cup water
- 1 tbsp lemon zest, grated
- 1 tbsp capers
- 1/2 cup basil, chopped
- 1 tbsp garlic, chopped
- 1 avocado, peeled and chopped
- Pepper
- Salt

Directions:

1. Add lemon zest, capers, basil, garlic, avocado, pepper, and salt into the blender blend until smooth.
2. Place fish fillets on aluminum foil and spread a blended mixture on fish fillets.
3. Fold foil around the fish fillets.
4. Pour water into the instant pot and place trivet in the pot.
5. Place foil fish packet on the trivet.
6. Seal pot with lid and cook on high for 8 minutes.
7. Once done, allow to release pressure naturally. Remove lid.
8. Serve and enjoy.

Nutritional Value (Amount per Serving):

- Calories 426
- Fat 16.6 g
- Carbohydrates 5.5 g
- Sugar 0.4 g
- Protein 61.8 g
- Cholesterol 93 mg

Delicious Lemon Butter Cod

Preparation Time: 10 minutes
Cooking Time: 8 minutes
Serve: 6

Ingredients:

- 1 1/2 lbs fresh cod fillets
- 28 oz can tomato, diced
- 1 tsp oregano
- 1 onion, sliced
- 1 lemon juice
- 3 tbsp butter
- Pepper
- Salt

Directions:

1. Add butter into the instant pot and set the pot on sauté mode.
2. Add onion and sauté for 5 minutes.
3. Add remaining ingredients and stir everything well.
4. Seal pot with lid and cook on high for 3 minutes.
5. Once done, release pressure using quick release. Remove lid.
6. Stir well and serve.

Nutritional Value (Amount per Serving):

- Calories 231
- Fat 6.9 g
- Carbohydrates 29 g
- Sugar 7.5 g
- Protein 14.7 g
- Cholesterol 51 mg

Quick & Easy Shrimp

Preparation Time: 10 minutes
Cooking Time: 1 minute
Serve: 6

Ingredients:

- 1 3/4 lbs shrimp, frozen and deveined
- 1/2 cup fish stock
- 1/2 cup apple cider vinegar
- Pepper
- Salt

Directions:

1. Add all ingredients into the inner pot of instant pot and stir well.
2. Seal pot with lid and cook on high for 1 minute.
3. Once done, release pressure using quick release. Remove lid.
4. Stir and serve.

Nutritional Value (Amount per Serving):

- Calories 165
- Fat 2.4 g
- Carbohydrates 2.2 g
- Sugar 0.1 g
- Protein 30.6 g
- Cholesterol 279 mg

Italian White Fish Fillets

Preparation Time: 10 minutes
Cooking Time: 4 minutes
Serve: 4

Ingredients:
- 4 white fish fillets, frozen
- 2 tbsp olive oil
- 1/3 cup roasted red peppers, sliced
- 2 tbsp capers
- 3/4 cup olives
- 3/4 cup cherry tomatoes
- 1/4 cup water
- 1/2 tsp salt

Directions:
1. Add water into the inner pot of instant pot then place fish fillets in the pot.
2. Pour remaining ingredients over fish fillets.
3. Seal pot with lid and cook on high for 4 minutes.
4. Once done, allow to release pressure naturally for 5 minutes then release remaining using quick release. Remove lid.
5. Serve and enjoy.

Nutritional Value (Amount per Serving):
- Calories 365
- Fat 21.4 g
- Carbohydrates 4 g
- Sugar 1.6 g
- Protein 38.4 g
- Cholesterol 119 mg

Shrimp Scampi

Preparation Time: 10 minutes
Cooking Time: 8 minutes
Serve: 6

Ingredients:
- 1 lb whole wheat penne pasta
- 1 lb frozen shrimp
- 2 tbsp garlic, minced
- 1/4 tsp cayenne
- 1/2 tbsp Italian seasoning
- 1/4 cup olive oil
- 3 1/2 cups fish stock
- Pepper
- Salt

Directions:
1. Add all ingredients into the inner pot of instant pot and stir well.
2. Seal pot with lid and cook on high for 6 minutes.
3. Once done, release pressure using quick release. Remove lid.
4. Stir well and serve.

Nutritional Value (Amount per Serving):
- Calories 435
- Fat 12.6 g
- Carbohydrates 54.9 g
- Sugar 0.1 g
- Protein 30.6 g
- Cholesterol 116 mg

Honey Garlic Shrimp

Preparation Time: 10 minutes
Cooking Time: 5 minutes
Serve: 4

Ingredients:
- 1 lb shrimp, peeled and deveined
- 1/4 cup honey
- 1 tbsp garlic, minced
- 1 tbsp ginger, minced
- 1 tbsp olive oil
- 1/4 cup fish stock
- Pepper
- Salt

Directions:
1. Add shrimp into the large bowl. Add remaining ingredients over shrimp and toss well.
2. Transfer shrimp into the instant pot and stir well.
3. Seal pot with lid and cook on high for 5 minutes.
4. Once done, release pressure using quick release. Remove lid.
5. Serve and enjoy.

Nutritional Value (Amount per Serving):
- Calories 240
- Fat 5.6 g
- Carbohydrates 20.9 g
- Sugar 17.5 g
- Protein 26.5 g
- Cholesterol 239 mg

Feta Tomato Sea Bass

Preparation Time: 10 minutes
Cooking Time: 8 minutes
Serve: 4

Ingredients:

- 4 sea bass fillets
- 1 1/2 cups water
- 1 tbsp olive oil
- 1 tsp garlic, minced
- 1 tsp basil, chopped
- 1 tsp parsley, chopped
- 1/2 cup feta cheese, crumbled
- 1 cup can tomatoes, diced
- Pepper
- Salt

Directions:

1. Season fish fillets with pepper and salt.
2. Pour 2 cups of water into the instant pot then place steamer rack in the pot.
3. Place fish fillets on steamer rack in the pot.
4. Seal pot with lid and cook on high for 5 minutes.
5. Once done, release pressure using quick release. Remove lid.
6. Remove fish fillets from the pot and clean the pot.
7. Add oil into the inner pot of instant pot and set the pot on sauté mode.
8. Add garlic and sauté for 1 minute.
9. Add tomatoes, parsley, and basil and stir well and cook for 1 minute.
10. Add fish fillets and top with crumbled cheese and cook for a minute.
11. Serve and enjoy.

Nutritional Value (Amount per Serving):

- Calories 219
- Fat 10.1 g
- Carbohydrates 4 g
- Sugar 2.8 g
- Protein 27.1 g
- Cholesterol 70 mg

Lemon Cod Peas

Preparation Time: 10 minutes
Cooking Time: 10 minutes
Serve: 4

Ingredients:

- 1 lb cod fillets, skinless, boneless and cut into chunks
- 1 cup fish stock
- 1 tbsp fresh parsley, chopped
- 1/2 tbsp lemon juice
- 1 green chili, chopped
- 3/4 cup fresh peas
- 2 tbsp onion, chopped
- Pepper
- Salt

Directions:

1. Add all ingredients into the inner pot of instant pot and stir well.
2. Seal pot with lid and cook on high for 10 minutes.
3. Once done, release pressure using quick release. Remove lid.
4. Stir and serve.

Nutritional Value (Amount per Serving):

- Calories 128
- Fat 1.6 g
- Carbohydrates 5 g
- Sugar 2.1 g
- Protein 23.2 g
- Cholesterol 41 mg

Spicy Tomato Crab Mix

Preparation Time: 10 minutes
Cooking Time: 12 minutes
Serve: 4

Ingredients:

- 1 lb crab meat
- 1 tsp paprika
- 1 cup grape tomatoes, cut into half
- 2 tbsp green onion, chopped
- 1 tbsp olive oil
- Pepper
- Salt

Directions:

1. Add oil into the inner pot of instant pot and set the pot on sauté mode.
2. Add paprika and onion and sauté for 2 minutes.
3. Add the rest of the ingredients and stir well.
4. Seal pot with lid and cook on high for 10 minutes.
5. Once done, release pressure using quick release. Remove lid.
6. Serve and enjoy.

Nutritional Value (Amount per Serving):

- Calories 142
- Fat 5.7 g
- Carbohydrates 4.3 g
- Sugar 1.3 g
- Protein 14.7 g
- Cholesterol 61 mg

Chili Lime Salmon

Preparation Time: 10 minutes
Cooking Time: 12 minutes
Serve: 4

Ingredients:

- 1 lb salmon, skinless, boneless, and cubed
- 1 cup fish stock
- 1 tbsp olive oil
- 1/2 tsp ground coriander
- 1/2 tbsp fresh lime juice
- 1 small onion, chopped
- 2 green chilies, chopped
- 1 tsp garlic, minced
- Pepper
- Salt

Directions:

1. Add oil into the inner pot of instant pot and set the pot on sauté mode.
2. Add garlic, onion, green chilies, and ground coriander and cook for 2 minutes.
3. Add remaining ingredients and stir well.
4. Seal pot with lid and cook on high for 10 minutes.
5. Once done, release pressure using quick release. Remove lid.
6. Stir well and serve.

Nutritional Value (Amount per Serving):

- Calories 200
- Fat 11 g
- Carbohydrates 2.5 g
- Sugar 0.9 g
- Protein 23.6 g
- Cholesterol 51 mg

Lemoney Prawns

Preparation Time: 10 minutes
Cooking Time: 3 minutes
Serve: 2

Ingredients:
- 1/2 lb prawns
- 1/2 cup fish stock
- 1 tbsp fresh lemon juice
- 1 tbsp lemon zest, grated
- 1 tbsp olive oil
- 1 tbsp garlic, minced
- Pepper
- Salt

Directions:
1. Add all ingredients into the inner pot of instant pot and stir well.
2. Seal pot with lid and cook on high for 3 minutes.
3. Once done, release pressure using quick release. Remove lid.
4. Drain prawns and serve.

Nutritional Value (Amount per Serving):
- Calories 215
- Fat 9.5 g
- Carbohydrates 3.9 g
- Sugar 0.4 g
- Protein 27.6 g
- Cholesterol 239 mg

Chapter 13: Desserts

Apple Dates Mix

Preparation Time: 10 minutes
Cooking Time: 15 minutes
Serve: 4

Ingredients:
- 4 apples, cored and cut into chunks
- 1 tsp vanilla
- 1 tsp cinnamon
- 1/2 cup dates, pitted
- 1 1/2 cups apple juice

Directions:
1. Add all ingredients into the inner pot of instant pot and stir well.
2. Seal pot with lid and cook on high for 15 minutes.
3. Once done, allow to release pressure naturally for 10 minutes then release remaining using quick release. Remove lid.
4. Stir and serve.

Nutritional Value (Amount per Serving):
- Calories 226
- Fat 0.6 g
- Carbohydrates 58.6 g
- Sugar 46.4 g
- Protein 1.3 g
- Cholesterol 0 mg

Fruit Nut Bowl

Preparation Time: 10 minutes
Cooking Time: 10 minutes
Serve: 2

Ingredients:

- 1/4 cup pecans, chopped
- 1/4 cup shredded coconut
- 1 cup of water
- 3 tbsp coconut oil
- 1/2 tsp cinnamon
- 1 pear, chopped
- 1 plum, chopped
- 2 tbsp Swerve
- 1 apple, chopped

Directions:

1. In a heat-safe dish add coconut, coconut oil, pear, apple, plum, and swerve and mix well.
2. Pour water into the instant pot then place the trivet in the pot.
3. Place dish on top of the trivet.
4. Seal pot with lid and cook on high for 10 minutes.
5. Once done, release pressure using quick release. Remove lid.
6. Remove dish from pot carefully. Top with pecans and serve.

Nutritional Value (Amount per Serving):

- Calories 338
- Fat 25.4 g
- Carbohydrates 47.2 g
- Sugar 37.6 g
- Protein 1.4 g
- Cholesterol 0 mg

Chocolate Nut Spread

Preparation Time: 10 minutes
Cooking Time: 10 minutes
Serve: 4

Ingredients:
- 1/4 cup unsweetened cocoa powder
- 1/4 tsp nutmeg
- 1 tsp vanilla
- 1/4 cup coconut oil
- 1 tsp liquid stevia
- 1/4 cup coconut cream
- 3 tbsp walnuts
- 1 cup almonds

Directions:
1. Add walnut and almonds into the food processor and process until smooth.
2. Add oil and process for 1 minute. Transfer to the bowl and stir in vanilla, nutmeg, and liquid stevia.
3. Add coconut cream into the instant pot and set the pot on sauté mode.
4. Add almond mixture and cocoa powder and stir well and cook for 5 minutes.
5. Pour into the container and store it in the refrigerator for 30 minutes.
6. Serve and enjoy.

Nutritional Value (Amount per Serving):
- Calories 342
- Fat 33.3 g
- Carbohydrates 9.6 g
- Sugar 1.8 g
- Protein 7.8 g
- Cholesterol 0 mg

Raisins Cinnamon Peaches

Preparation Time: 10 minutes
Cooking Time: 15 minutes
Serve: 4

Ingredients:

- 4 peaches, cored and cut into chunks
- 1 tsp vanilla
- 1 tsp cinnamon
- 1/2 cup raisins
- 1 cup of water

Directions:

1. Add all ingredients into the inner pot of instant pot and stir well.
2. Seal pot with lid and cook on high for 15 minutes.
3. Once done, allow to release pressure naturally for 10 minutes then release remaining using quick release. Remove lid.
4. Stir and serve.

Nutritional Value (Amount per Serving):

- Calories 118
- Fat 0.5 g
- Carbohydrates 29 g
- Sugar 24.9 g
- Protein 2 g
- Cholesterol 0 mg

Choco Rice Pudding

Preparation Time: 10 minutes
Cooking Time: 20 minutes
Serve: 4

Ingredients:
- 1 1/4 cup rice
- 1/4 cup dark chocolate, chopped
- 1 tsp vanilla
- 1/3 cup coconut butter
- 1 tsp liquid stevia
- 2 1/2 cups almond milk

Directions:
1. Add all ingredients into the inner pot of instant pot and stir well.
2. Seal pot with lid and cook on high for 20 minutes.
3. Once done, allow to release pressure naturally. Remove lid.
4. Stir well and serve.

Nutritional Value (Amount per Serving):
- Calories 632
- Fat 39.9 g
- Carbohydrates 63.5 g
- Sugar 12.5 g
- Protein 8.6 g
- Cholesterol 2 mg

Healthy Zucchini Pudding

Preparation Time: 10 minutes
Cooking Time: 10 minutes
Serve: 4

Ingredients:
- 2 cups zucchini, shredded
- 1/4 tsp cardamom powder
- 5 oz half and half
- 5 oz almond milk
- 1/4 cup Swerve

Directions:
1. Add all ingredients except cardamom into the instant pot and stir well.
2. Seal pot with lid and cook on high for 10 minutes.
3. Once done, allow to release pressure naturally for 10 minutes then release remaining using quick release. Remove lid.
4. Stir in cardamom and serve.

Nutritional Value (Amount per Serving):
- Calories 137
- Fat 12.6 g
- Carbohydrates 20.5 g
- Sugar 17.2 g
- Protein 2.6 g
- Cholesterol 13 mg

Coconut Risotto Pudding

Preparation Time: 10 minutes
Cooking Time: 20 minutes
Serve: 6

Ingredients:
- 3/4 cup rice
- 1/2 cup shredded coconut
- 1 tsp lemon juice
- 1/2 tsp vanilla
- 14.5 oz can coconut milk
- 1/4 cup maple syrup
- 1 1/2 cups water

Directions:
1. Add all ingredients into the instant pot and stir well.
2. Seal pot with lid and cook on high for 20 minutes.
3. Once done, allow to release pressure naturally for 10 minutes then release remaining using quick release. Remove lid.
4. Blend pudding mixture using an immersion blender until smooth.
5. Serve and enjoy.

Nutritional Value (Amount per Serving):
- Calories 205
- Fat 8.6 g
- Carbohydrates 29.1 g
- Sugar 9 g
- Protein 2.6 g
- Cholesterol 0 mg

Strawberry Stew

Preparation Time: 10 minutes
Cooking Time: 15 minutes
Serve: 4

Ingredients:
- 12 oz fresh strawberries, sliced
- 1 tsp vanilla
- 1 1/2 cups water
- 1 tsp liquid stevia
- 2 tbsp lime juice

Directions:
1. Add all ingredients into the inner pot of instant pot and stir well.
2. Seal pot with lid and cook on high for 15 minutes.
3. Once done, allow to release pressure naturally for 10 minutes then release remaining using quick release. Remove lid.
4. Stir and serve.

Nutritional Value (Amount per Serving):
- Calories 36
- Fat 0.3 g
- Carbohydrates 8.5 g
- Sugar 4.7 g
- Protein 0.7 g
- Cholesterol 0 mg

Tapioca Pudding

Preparation Time: 10 minutes
Cooking Time: 10 minutes
Serve: 4

Ingredients:

- 2 1/2 cups almond milk
- 1 tsp cinnamon
- 1 tsp liquid stevia
- 1/2 cup quinoa
- 1/3 cup tapioca pearls, rinsed
- Pinch of salt

Directions:

1. Spray instant pot from inside with cooking spray.
2. Add all ingredients into the inner pot of instant pot and stir well.
3. Seal pot with lid and cook on high for 10 minutes.
4. Once done, allow to release pressure naturally for 10 minutes then release remaining using quick release. Remove lid.
5. Stir well and serve.

Nutritional Value (Amount per Serving):

- Calories 470
- Fat 37.1 g
- Carbohydrates 33.7 g
- Sugar 5.4 g
- Protein 6.5 g
- Cholesterol 0 mg

Blackberry Jam

Preparation Time: 10 minutes
Cooking Time: 6 hours
Serve: 6

Ingredients:
- 3 cups fresh blackberries
- 1/4 cup chia seeds
- 4 tbsp Swerve
- 1/4 cup fresh lemon juice
- 1/4 cup coconut butter

Directions:
1. Add all ingredients into the instant pot and stir well.
2. Seal the pot with a lid and select slow cook mode and cook on low for 6 hours.
3. Pour in container and store in fridge.

Nutritional Value (Amount per Serving):
- Calories 101
- Fat 6.8 g
- Carbohydrates 20 g
- Sugar 14.4 g
- Protein 2 g
- Cholesterol 0 mg

Spiced Pear Sauce

Preparation Time: 10 minutes
Cooking Time: 6 hours
Serve: 12

Ingredients:
- 8 pears, cored and diced
- 1/2 tsp ground cinnamon
- 1/4 tsp ground nutmeg
- 1/4 tsp ground cardamom
- 1 cup of water

Directions:
1. Add all ingredients into the instant pot and stir well.
2. Seal the pot with a lid and select slow cook mode and cook on low for 6 hours.
3. Mash the sauce using potato masher.
4. Pour into the container and store it in the fridge.

Nutritional Value (Amount per Serving):
- Calories 81
- Fat 0.2 g
- Carbohydrates 21.4 g
- Sugar 13.6 g
- Protein 0.5 g
- Cholesterol 0 mg

Conclusion

Delicious and easy home cooking that promotes health and weight loss doesn't have to be difficult or involve bland and boring meals. With the goal of making a ketogenic Mediterranean lifestyle accessible and convenient for everyone, Ketogenic Mediterranean Diet Cookbook combines healthy low-carb recipes with the age old wisdom from one of the healthiest and best tasting diets, the Mediterranean diet. This Cookbook is the first choice for busy home cooks who just want to enjoy delicious and healthy recipes that are simple to prep, cook, and enjoy at home whether alone or with friends and family!

Say goodbye to choosing between unhealthy takeout or spending all your free time in the kitchen. Now you have healthy and delicious meals you can make at home with the Ketogenic Mediterranean Diet Cookbook, your go-to resource for making the ketogenic Mediterranean diet a successful and enjoyable experience!

www.ingramcontent.com/pod-product-compliance
Lightning Source LLC
Chambersburg PA
CBHW081400070526
44583CB00020B/2617